THE **SECRET SIGNS** THE **UNIVERSE** WANTS YOU TO KNOW

When the Going Gets Tough,
Have a Little Faith!

Third Edition

A N D R E W   K A N I A S

Copyright © 2023 Andrew Kanias.

All rights reserved. No part of this book may be used or reproduced by any means, graphic, electronic, or mechanical, including photocopying, recording, taping or by any information storage retrieval system without the written permission of the author except in the case of brief quotations embodied in critical articles and reviews.

Balboa Press books may be ordered through booksellers or by contacting:

Balboa Press
A Division of Hay House
1663 Liberty Drive
Bloomington, IN 47403
www.balboapress.co.uk
UK TFN: 0800 0148647 (Toll Free inside the UK)
UK Local: 02036 956325 (+44 20 3695 6325 from outside the UK)

Because of the dynamic nature of the Internet, any web addresses or links contained in this book may have changed since publication and may no longer be valid. The views expressed in this work are solely those of the author and do not necessarily reflect the views of the publisher, and the publisher hereby disclaims any responsibility for them.

Any people depicted in stock imagery provided by Getty Images are models, and such images are being used for illustrative purposes only. Certain stock imagery © Getty Images.

ISBN: 978-1-9822-8599-9 (sc)
ISBN: 978-1-9822-8600-2 (e)

Print information available on the last page.

Balboa Press rev. date: 01/19/2023

Email: TheSecretSigns@hotmail.com
Facebook Page: The Secret Signs the Universe Wants You to Know
Instagram: @TheSecretSignsBook

BALBOA.PRESS
A DIVISION OF HAY HOUSE

I dedicate this book to my family, who have always supported
and believed in me throughout my struggles.

In memory of

Theodosis William Dixon
10 October 1960–20 November 2017

and

Tony Tsiappouli (Chaps)
25 June 1964–7 June 2021

Contents

When It All Started

In 1993, when I was twenty-three, I suffered what my sister described as a nervous breakdown. To me, it was the beginning of the most horrendous time of my life.

I was in my final year of university and had all sorts of fears and worries going on in my mind. These fears and worries eventually led to severe panic attacks and depression, which took me years to overcome.

Over the years, I learned to control the anxiety through natural methods such as meditation, relaxation, visualisation, neuro linguistic programming (NLP), positive thinking, and affirmations.

However, seven years ago, when life was going better than ever, I had a reoccurrence of severe anxiety. It was a difficult time.

The date was Thursday, 10 September 2015, and I was locking up by myself after one of my karate classes. I remember it clearly because it was my niece's birthday, and I was heading to a restaurant to celebrate.

As I left the large, empty school hall after closing up, I felt a tickle in my throat. I coughed. And then I coughed harder. And then I coughed again even harder. It wouldn't go away.

I shoved all my bags containing karate equipment into the car and drove out of the double iron gates before padlocking them. Behind me, the darkening sky added to my apprehension.

The tickle in my throat was still there, and I kept coughing and coughing, but it wouldn't go away. I began to lose my breath. My heart rate increased, and I bent over in an attempt to recover. I looked around for help, but there was no one there, only the silence of the upper-class, residential road. I gasped and felt as though I was about to die. And no one would know.

Still bent over by the iron gates, I coughed one last time with all my might, and that's when I felt the panic grow inside me like a tidal wave rising on a quiet ocean. It was a panic that was all too familiar to me. And as I thought to myself, *This is the end*, I somehow found my breath again and began to breathe, shallowly. The tickle had gone, and I felt as though I was going to be okay.

The incident shattered my confidence and was the beginning of another two-year battle to overcome anxiety. What happened next is documented in this book: I found a renewed strength and confidence and the ability to live a happy life.

I went from being anxious about absolutely everything to achieving some lifelong goals such as speaking on stage to more than a thousand people, giving online talks, working as an artist, writing, competing in tennis tournaments, and even going for an audition for an acting role. And I got back to enjoying all the things I so missed, like watching a good film in the cinema, competing in karate, traveling, and going to the gym.

I'm not saying I'm now a daredevil. I still wouldn't bungee Jump, jump from a plane with a parachute, or climb Everest. It's about doing the simple things in life so many of us don't do because of our fears, negative thoughts, or limiting beliefs. And my wish for you is that this book will

- help you to overcome challenges,
- help comfort you in times of need,
- help you to let go of fears,
- guide you to achieve your true potential, and
- bring peace and meaning into your life.

Declaration

Before we get into this book, I would like to clarify a few things.

This book is not religious and does not aim to question whether God exists or not. It is simply a reference book for those who seek guidance in their lives and are, like me, spiritual but not necessarily deeply religious.

Personally, I do believe in God and was born into a Greek Orthodox family; I practice this faith but not religiously.

I will sometimes be referring to God as I will the universe. And I'll often refer to angels and spirit guides. I believe there is a higher power, but I do not hold all the answers.

I would also like to mention that I am spiritual but have never seen an angel, a guide, or a ghost. I do, however, believe in them.

I am not a clairvoyant or psychic, but I believe I was called to write this book.

I do not set out to be controversial or dispel anybody else's belief in anything in particular.

Finally, I have included stories of self-healing and miracles but am not making any medical claims.

I have written this book in order to help others as I was helped by everything I talk about.

That being said, please have an open mind and enjoy

The Man and the Flood

A terrible storm came into a town, and local officials sent out an emergency warning that the riverbanks would soon overflow and flood the nearby homes. They ordered everyone in the town to evacuate immediately.

A faithful Christian man heard the warning and decided to stay, saying to himself, "I will trust God, and if I am in danger, then God will send a divine miracle to save me."

The neighbours came by his house and said to him, "We're leaving and there is room for you in our car; please come with us."

But the man declined. "I have faith that God will save me."

As the man stood on his porch watching the water rise up the steps, a man in a canoe paddled by and called to him, "Hurry and come into my canoe; the waters are rising quickly."

But the man again said, "No thanks, God will save me."

The floodwaters rose higher, pouring water into his living room, and the man had to retreat to the second floor. A police motorboat came by and saw him at the window.

"We will come up and rescue you," they shouted.

But the man refused and waved them off, saying, "Use your time to save someone else. I have faith that God will save me."

The flood waters rose higher and higher, and the man had to climb up to his rooftop.

A helicopter spotted him and dropped a rope ladder. A rescue officer came down the ladder and pleaded with the man, "Grab my hand, and I will pull you up."

But the man still refused, folding his arms tightly to his body. "No, thank you. God will save me."

Shortly after, the house broke up, and the floodwaters swept the man away, and he drowned.

When in heaven, the man stood before God and asked, "I put all of my faith in You. Why didn't You come and save me?"

And God said, "Son, I sent you a warning. I sent you a car. I sent you a canoe. I sent you a motorboat. I sent you a helicopter. What more were you looking for?"

This story from an unknown source is a typical example of people receiving guidance from God (or the universe) but never noticing it.

What Are You Looking For?

Signs are everywhere, if you only just believe and open your eyes, ears, and, of course, your nose. On car registration plates, in the sky, on the floor, on television, on clocks, on receipts, in the trees, in a sunset, in a song, in the ocean, in a film, and so on.

I believe that from the moment we get up in the morning to the moment we go to bed, we are shown the way. But our minds are just too busy and occupied with thoughts to see what's right there in front of us.

Too many people go through life without stopping to appreciate each day for what it is, a gift; they lose track of why they are really here. Have you ever stopped to think about your true purpose in life?

Is it to work nine to five for forty years in a job you don't like? To live from wage packet to wage packet, unable to afford your dream holiday? Or to commute for hours a day in the rush-hour traffic?

Obviously, no one chooses to do this voluntarily, but so many get stuck in a routine like this. They never get to do what they truly came here to do.

Like to become a writer, or to help people get healthier, or to travel the world, or to become a musician.

Take time to think about this, and if you're really happy, I mean, really happy, then that's fine. But if there's more calling you, then ask the universe for a sign, for guidance, and to help you discover the person you really should be.

Sadly, it's said that 97 percent of people in the world never live to achieve their full potential, for all sorts of reasons. The main one is fear: fear of failure, fear of success, fear of stepping out of their comfort circle, or fear of fear itself.

Everyone has a choice, either to step forward into growth or to step backwards into safety. What have you chosen?

If you believe you are here to achieve more in life, my message to you is have faith, trust the process, and go for it.

Later, I will explain what you need to do in order to step forward into growth and become the person you so desire, but first, let me briefly explain why I wrote this book.

Why I Wrote This Book

When my anxiety resurfaced seven years ago, I decided to get serious with my methods of overcoming it. I was desperate to find a way to really kick anxiety into touch.

I began to read spiritual books in my quest to find the answers to my problems and came across a good book by Theresa Cheung called *The Ten Secrets of Heaven*. This led me to other books such as Anita Moorjani's amazing story, *Dying to Be Me*. Both gave me great hope and, more importantly, belief that everything would be okay.

I began to receive signs and felt like I was being helped and supported by angels and other heavenly beings, like saints.

The more I believed, the more I would ask for guidance, and the more signs I seemed to receive.

My faith became stronger, and using some good techniques to control my anxiety, I began to feel better again.

And that's when I began to see, feel, and hear messages in the forms I talk about in this book. They came thick and fast: treble numbers, feathers, high-pitched sounds, birds flying past me, hearts, falling leaves.

And they always came when I least expected them. I would have dismissed them, but they seemed to come at the exact moment my mind would be thinking of something significant, like, *Am I going to be okay?*

I would see 777s on car registration plates or 11:11 on my phone. It became too obvious to be coincidence, and that's when I began to believe that these signs were significant.

For the last seven years or so, a day has not gone by without me seeing multiple and treble numbers numerous times.

Along with other methods of healing, I have overcome anxiety, and I believe I'm totally in control for the first time.

I am so passionate about this subject that I want to share it with the world. The only thing I ask is, have an open mind, even if you are sceptical. Just follow what I believe will help you to open up to the signs, smells, and numbers, and your prayers will be answered. Trust me.

Open Your Mind to the Signs

Many people will say, "Okay, so I guess I have to meditate for hours a day to be able to receive and see the signs." Not true.

You do, however, need to slow down a little, go with the flow more, trust the process, and be open-minded. If you believe, you will receive. I recommend you practice the following simple steps regularly, daily if possible, or just pick one to work with each day. Perhaps number 1 on Sundays, number 2 on Mondays, number 3 on Tuesdays, and so on.

Before all this stuff began to happen to me, I was the kind of person who tried to do everything, all at the same time. I would juggle a life of hobbies, studying, writing, and running two businesses, never pausing to enjoy the moment. I would get stressed and annoyed, having no time for my family and friends.

Now, I tend to trust everything will happen in good time, without me worrying. I set my intention, go with the flow, and think positive. Lo and behold, even though I am now seemingly spinning more plates than ever before, I have so much more time. And my businesses are a greater success because of it.

The universe somehow managed to get my attention, and I decided it was time to make serious changes. Apart from my decision to meditate daily (more on this later), I took action to lessen the load weekly. I managed to free up around eight hours of my working week and still got paid the same. Of course, I made other crucial changes, most of them minor, and began to listen more to my intuition.

I believe the following steps are a good start to living a better, happier life. Most of the steps are a change in mind-set.

I call them the seven Gs.

1. Be Grateful for everything.

Be grateful for your life. Be grateful for the day. Be grateful for your bed. Be grateful for the house you live in. Be grateful for the food you eat. Be grateful for your health. Be grateful for your job. Be grateful to people who are always there for you. Get the idea? You can practice gratitude anywhere: while on your way to work, before you get out of bed in the morning, before you go to sleep at night, or when waiting in a queue. You can also choose to write it down in a journal.

2. Be Good to yourself.

Learn to be good to yourself, and start saying positive affirmations to help stop negative thoughts. Many of us say things like, "I'm useless," or "I always mess up," or even "I'm an idiot." How would you react if your best friend spoke to you like that? Obviously, you wouldn't be happy, so why do you give yourself permission to do so? Years of negative talk eventually took its toll on me, and I had a nervous breakdown before realising how hard I was on myself. Don't be like me. Take control, and know you have control over your thoughts. Here are two affirmations I took from Susan Jeffers's excellent book, *Dare to Connect*:

> No matter how anyone reacts to me, I know I am a worthwhile person.

> I am good enough exactly as I am…and who I am is a powerful and loving human being who is learning and growing every step of the way.

3. Ask for Guidance.

As you quiet your mind, begin to ask for guidance and signs in order to help you on your journey. Be open to hearing advice while in this silence. Trust me, it does come eventually, even if it takes weeks or months. Be patient.

4. Write down your Goals.

Write a list of goals you want to achieve, like travelling, buying your dream house, or finding love. Read them each day or record your voice and play them back as you travel to work. Don't limit yourself on this. Write down a hundred if you want.

5. Go with the flow.

Trust the process. If things irritate you, learn to accept them as part of the process that will help you to become a better person and achieve your goals. Don't worry if this is hard to do at first. It all takes a little practice, like learning to ride a bike.

Deepak Chopra said it well in his book *The Seven Spiritual Laws of Success*. One of the laws is the "Law of Least Effort." And this law is based on the fact that nature's intelligence functions with effortless ease. So shouldn't we, as human beings, be the same?

6. Know that God is working with you.

Trust that God or the universe wants you to succeed or, if you have health issues, to get better. Have an unwavering belief you will achieve everything you desire.

7. Don't Gossip. Send love instead.

At the risk of sounding like a hippy, my advice is to send love to people everywhere, instead of judgement. Send love to that person who is homeless. Send love to the man who cut you off on the road. Send love to that person you don't get on with in the family. Send love to that lady walking down the street who looks worried. Send love.

The universe works better with you when you send love.

The seven Gs are:

1) Be **Grateful.**
2) Be **Good** to yourself.
3) Ask for **Guidance.**
4) Write down your **Goals.**
5) **Go** with the flow.
6) **God** is working with you.
7) Don't **Gossip**. Send love instead.

By the way, this book was not on my fifteen-year life plan. It just happened. If someone had asked me to write this (other than God), I probably would have said, "Er, no, I haven't got time." But with so many strange things happening to me, I felt compelled to let others know.

At first, I spoke to my friends and family, most of whom thought I was a bit crazy. However, there were a few who related with me and began to have similar experiences. It got to the point it all seemed so ridiculous and laughable, I thought I'd write a small book as a bit of a joke between us.

People loved it and said I should publish it. So I asked more and more people to read it for their opinions. I wanted the most sceptical people to read it too, people I knew would tell me the truth. All came back with positive words, some with constructive advice.

The best part was how it helped so many people. They explained they'd been seeing things for years and never realised they could be signs of support. So they began to believe, and this encouraged me to publish it. My hope is, so many people will benefit and start to believe that we are not alone here.

Whatever challenges you are now facing, maybe you too should take a step back and re-examine everything. The seven Gs are a good starting point.

Signs You Will Receive

So what exactly is a sign from heaven? Is it a beautiful cloud shaped like an angel? Is it tiny white feather falling from the sky? Or is it an interesting sequence of numbers or letters found on a street sign?

Actually, it's all of those and many, many more.

Signs come in all forms, way too many to mention in this book. The universe rules and can send us signs unique to us and us only. However, the most common signs our human brain is capable of receiving are listed in this book. I've experienced all of these. And probably so many more I never noticed.

Chances are, as you read through this book, you will begin to receive signs in many forms. Please, please share this with us on your social media and use the hashtag #MySecretSign.

Numbers

Although I have used treble numbers, single or double numbers have the same meaning. It's also easier to notice treble numbers and awe-inspiring at the same time.

I could include hundreds of stories that have personally happened to me over the last few years, but I have chosen the most memorable one to share with you. It's one of the most miraculous I've experienced in terms of noticing numbers and occurred in July 2016, when I was travelling to Eastbourne for a karate training camp with some of my students.

We had been driving for around three hours when it happened. The car mileage meter was showing 33325 (nearing 33,333 miles) when I noticed the amount of petrol in the tank available: 335 miles. I mentioned it to the others, and we joked how amazing it would be if they coincided. As I continued to drive, the petrol tank meter dropped gradually to 329 as the mileage of the car increased to 33,330, so it wasn't likely to happen. However, to our amazement, the petrol reading suddenly began to rise instead of fall. As we got closer to 33,333 miles, the petrol meter kept rising until it got to 333 the same moment we hit 33,333. It was unbelievable. This had never happened before; the petrol meter changing direction. I never changed the way I was driving, and we were still on the same road in Eastbourne, so there was no reason for this to happen.

Over the years, numbers, and especially treble numbers, have become something of a comforting sign to me. When loved ones of mine have been unwell or in hospital, or if I was worried about anything, multiple numbers appeared to me in abundance. It's as if they were assuring me that everything was going to be okay, which it always was.

I've also noticed that when I am extremely happy and everything is going my way, I see more signs than ever, as if God is letting me know I'm on the right track and is pleased for me.

Note, the meanings to the numbers I give below are not the same as other sources you may find in books and websites. This is because the meanings were personal to me, and I have linked affirmations to the numbers.

I believe that whatever meaning you give to a number or whatever source you use to translate it, that's the meaning that is intended for you. So don't worry about this. The universe has it all sorted.

000

New Beginnings. Great things are coming your way. Each day is a chance to start again and the chance to make your dreams come true.

Reminds you to accept things as they are and to trust that it is all for the best.

Affirmation
Great things are coming my way, and I am so happy and grateful.

111

Harmony and Oneness. Think positive. What you focus on most is manifesting. Trust the process, and go with the flow. Be at one with the universe.

This number is a reminder that your thoughts are powerfully manifesting, so make sure they are positive.

Affirmation
The universe is working with me to succeed.

222

Love and Forgiveness. You are loved. Love yourself, and others will too. Love also those you may not be getting on with. Love heals.

A nudge from the angels to love and appreciate yourself more and to send love out. Send love silently to those around you at this moment.

Affirmation
I am powerful, and I am loved.

333

Faith and Belief. Your heavenly beings are always with you. Have complete faith you will achieve all you desire, including overcoming any health issues.

Visualise yourself succeeding. Have complete faith and belief you will overcome challenges. Accept everything.

Affirmation
I accept everything that happens to me. I trust my mind, body, and soul to deal with it naturally, and I am at total peace with myself.

444

Happiness and Joy. Be present in the moment. Don't worry about the future. Don't dwell on the past. See the beauty in everything right now. Happiness is a choice.

Live in the present moment, and really appreciate what you already have.

Affirmation
My mind is calm, and I think positive and happy thoughts at all times and in any situation.

555

Strength and Courage. Face your fears, knowing the higher power is with you. Surrender to God, knowing that whatever happens, it is all for the best. Fortune favours the brave.

A message from above to be strong at this particular time. You are being comforted.

Affirmation
I have the courage and strength to continue on my desired journey, knowing great things are coming.

666

Change and Shift in Balance. Trust changes in your life will work out for the best. This may include some kind of loss, a big move, or a new career path.

Change is for a good reason. Don't doubt it. Balance will be restored very soon.

Affirmation
My life is changing for the better.

777

Spiritual and Healing. A spiritual calling to help others or to do some kind of spiritual work, such as helping the homeless, a healing job, caring for someone, or even to pursue a creative job, such as music or writing.

You are spiritual, and you can make a significant change to someone's life, maybe even the world.

Affirmation
I am full of radiant good health, healing energy, vitality, and a strong immune system.

888

Abundance, Wealth, and Prosperity. You will succeed. Keep going, no matter what other people say. Stay focused.

Confirmation that whatever you're working on or thinking about at the very moment you see this number, you will succeed doing it, especially with regards to money, a new job, or career change.

Affirmation
I am successful doing what I love.

999

Help, Support, and Guidance. Support is at hand, from the angels, the universe, or people here on earth. Any suffering is coming to an end.

Letting you know you are never alone. Ask for guidance, and listen.

Affirmation
God and my heavenly companions protect me, heal me, and guide me in the right direction. Help to create miracles and other great things in and around my life.

Other Common Number Sequences

123, 456, 789, 321, 654, 987, 246, 369

If you are noticing numbers similar to these, they may have a combined meaning.

For instance, if you notice 101 a lot, it could be the universe telling you that you are starting on a new project and to remember to have faith. The universe has your back.

In Kyle Gray's book, *Raise Your Vibration*, he states that seeing number sequences like 1234 and 6789, and times like 12:34, means you are taking the right steps to lift your heart and energy; you are making a positive change to the world.

A good task to try one day is to jot down all the numbered signs you see, without obsessively looking for them. You might be surprised how many you come up with.

One particular number sequence I keep seeing, almost every day, is 177 and 117. Sometimes, it could even be 11:17 on the clock or 17:17. This usually happens when I'm thinking or talking about a loved one who has passed on.

I have come to believe my spirit guides are with me when I see these numbers. What numbers could be personal to you?

You may also dream of certain numbers and sequences. It may not be the winning lottery numbers, but they could be significant. In fact, just the other day, I dreamt that I saw the numbers 17:17 on a clock. More on dreams later.

The Clock Talks to You

One day, I went to see what all the fuss was about when a miraculous icon of the Virgin Mary came to our town from Hawaii. It was said to leak a sweet, scented oil, like myrrh, from the wood it was painted on.

I was extremely sceptical. To say I was dumfounded is an understatement. The myrrh didn't just drip from the icon; it poured nonstop. So much so, it's kept in a casing which needs large amounts of cotton wool below it in order to capture the oil.

I was so excited about this; I had the sudden urge to tell two of my close friends, who were on a similar spiritual journey to me.

I left the church in haste, took out my iPhone to call them, and to my shock and disbelief, the exact time was 11:11. It was as though God was telling me, "See, miracles do happen."

See Resources at the end of the book for the YouTube video link that talks about this miraculous icon.

My point is that the clock display, especially in the modern world of smartphones, holds so much in terms of signs of assurance and messages. You just have to be open to it.

The meaning could be personal or universal. It all depends on how you receive the message and at what moment.

You may also see these clock sequences on Facebook posts and comments, texts, receipts, emails, and anything else that has a time on it.

Check out my Instagram profile @andrew_kanias for the many great photos of signs I have collected over the years.

Remember, the meaning could be personal to you, or you can use the guide above to interpret them, whatever feels right at the time.

For instance, when I saw 11:11 in the example, it wasn't the first time. In fact, this sequence had been showing itself to me and my two friends for some months before this happened. So when it appeared to me at that very moment, it seemed highly miraculous. So the message I took from this was, "Believe more."

Many popular spiritualists write that there are no coincidences in life, and I am inclined to agree with them.

You may also see number sequences like 12:21. This may be a message that you should go with the flow and forgive someone you may actually be thinking about at that precise moment.

The key is this: Whatever you're thinking at the time of the sign, see if you can make sense of it. Most of the time, it will probably make no sense, but take it as a reassurance that if you are worried about something, all will work out for the best in the end. Have faith.

Clock Number Sequences You May See

11:11, 22:22, 09:09, 10:10, 12:12, 12:21

21:12, 14:44, 12:22, 13:33, 15:15, 17:17

12:34 (1234), 14:23 (1234 in anagram form)

23:45, 00:00, 01:11, 02:22, 03:33, 04:44

The list is endless.

I would like to add one more thing with regards to seeing number sequences on clocks and car odometers. As much as they can be awe-inspiring, they're also a reminder that time doesn't stand still, and neither does the journey to our destination. It will always keep moving, and the moment you see something like 11:11 on the display, one minute later, it's 11:12. Gone.

I believe it's a message to keep moving forward, to keep going for your dreams, to have a sense of urgency at all times and make every second count, to remember that when you actually do achieve that almighty dream of yours, moments after, it's in the past, and you need a new destination. Be prepared for that. Never stop growing, and have a goal in mind ready for when you do eventually achieve that which you so desire.

So many people have dreams and goals they want to achieve, and they will often say, "I will achieve it someday." Yet they will never take the first steps. They are too busy waiting for the right time, the perfect time, when everything is going swimmingly, and they can put their full attention towards it. This is the biggest myth of all.

How often do you hear of a person's journey to success and how they achieved it despite adversity? I cannot ever remember reading any success stories that were easily achieved without some kind of chaos or obstacles. Usually, it's the chaos and obstacles that fuel the determination to succeed.

The message is, time waits for no one. Take the first steps now, and stop worrying what other people might say and stop saying, "Someday."

Letters and Words

Letter sequences, words, and names you see regularly can have a significant meaning. Is there a message for you somewhere?

For instance, on car registration plates:

AAA, BBB GGG, ZZZ, ABC, BOB

GOD, LOV, GO, UP, SEE, LIV

Or they could just be assuring you that God is with you.

This happened to me recently:

I was driving along the motorway, listening to one of my favourite spiritual writers, Dr Wayne W. Dyer, on Audible. The audio was called "Mastering the Present Moment," and Dr Wayne spoke a lot about the Taoist Master, Lao Tzu, and his amazing philosophy. I was wowed by the teachings when I suddenly noticed a car overtaking me and, in particular, its registration number. The last three letters, separate from the first three digits, read TZU.

Maybe the universe was assuring me that the teachings were to be taken seriously.

Another incident happened that left me awestruck:

It was just a few weeks after my beloved godbrother passed away suddenly. Tony, known as Chaps by his close friends and family, was the kind of person who always made people laugh with his unique cockney humour and happy-go-lucky attitude to life.

I was working as a supporting artist on a television show; after a long day of filming, I entered the changing rooms to remove my costume. There was a small white feather on the floor near the clothes rack, but I didn't think too much of it because I always see them. As I took my costume trousers off to wear my jeans, I looked down to notice the word written on the back of them: CHAPS! My eyes widened, and I was in shock for a few moments before smiling, knowing it was a sign from him, along with the white feather, that he was doing just fine in spirit.

When I was a teenager, Tony took me to my first-ever football match at White Hart Lane to watch Tottenham Hotspur. I remember it clearly. It was a rainy day, but that didn't dampen our spirits, as our team drew. It was the first time I'd ever stepped out onto the terraces to the beautiful aroma of fresh grass wafting in the breeze.

Another common occurrence, and far too often to be coincidence, is what I call word synchronicity. This happens to me when I'm reading a book, for instance, and the television's on in the background. A word I'll read (or even two or three words) is suddenly said at the exact time on the TV.

It may also happen to me whilst I'm driving with the radio on, and I notice a word on a car (or sign) the DJ speaks at that exact moment. Or if I'm in a café, and I hear someone say a word I suddenly see whilst scrolling through social media.

Has something like this happened to you in the past that you were quick to dispel as coincidence?

Birds

I never thought of birds as messengers before, but this was something I became aware of too. A single bird flying past my car windscreen in close proximity. Sometimes, it would get so close, I thought I would hit it.

Or a large flock of birds flying low. It was as though I'd be thinking about something in particular, and then they would fly by. Or I'd be worried about the health of a loved one when a flock of birds would appear.

It became a regular occurrence, and it still happens. Whether I'm walking or driving, I often notice birds around me, whether they're high above in the sky or close to me. Before, I can't say I ever noticed. I was oblivious to them. Now, I even notice the shadow of a bird cast on the ground when it passes the sun.

Have you ever stopped to watch a bird flying through the air? Effortlessly swooping down to make a landing, working hard to ascend into the sky, or glide through the air enjoying its freedom? It can be an extremely beautiful sight and meditative too.

A dear cousin of mine passed away recently, and at his funeral, seven white doves were released into the sky. I filmed the moment on my mobile phone from a distance. I couldn't believe it when the birds flew off together in their beautiful formation, spun around, and flew directly over our heads.

I often think of birds as angels bringing us messages from above.

Robins

Robins are known to be truly spiritual birds. So when you see one, know that someone from the other side is speaking to you, letting you know they're alright.

I recently went to see a psychic reader for the first time ever. Rhian, or Psychicmaiden as she is known online, was recommended to me by a friend. The first reading went well, so I decided to go again, six months later.

While Rhian was reading my cards, I saw the most beautiful little robin fly onto a tree outside in her garden. I never said anything until the end, but Rhian confirmed this was a highly good, spiritual sign.

In early 2018, the Greek community of Cardiff lost a well-respected and popular member of its community to a dreadful disease which affects the heart. Anastasis, or Tasos, as everyone affectionately called him, was a barber and played the bouzouki at local events and parties as far back as I can remember.

It was a great shock to us all and especially to his dear family. But one thing happened that, for me, cannot be explained as coincidence is that while his close family were at a family-owned field, a robin came out of nowhere to them. And for weeks, it hung around and ate seeds from their hands. Tasos's mum was one of those people it went to.

Antony has another wonderful story (in his own words):

> Robins have always featured in my life during times of loss, and although I believe their significance, I don't always believe. But on one occasion, it was too obvious to be coincidence.
>
> It was my daughter's baby's christening, and there were around sixty of us in the garden, celebrating with music, food, and drink. There were balloons everywhere too, and it certainly wasn't quiet. In fact, quite the opposite. And out of the blue, a robin came along and sat on the fence, as if it was watching us. I believe this was one of our dearly departed loved ones.

Flowers

Flowers are often taken for granted. We rush around with our busy lives, forgetting they even exist. They add the most beautiful colours to our world, often calming. Their fragrant aromas are used to scent perfumes and relaxing essential oils.

If you're seeing or smelling certain flowers, could it be a sign personal to you?

Remember, when a flower blooms, it doesn't bloom for long before it's gone, so take time to appreciate it. It may be your spirit guides comforting you.

Cherry blossoming is a highly cherished event in Japan, and they have many famous destinations like Yoshino, Kansai, where thousands flock to visit in spring. In mid-April, the blossoms of thousands of cherry trees create a floral layer that ascend into the mountains.

I love this quote spoken by Samurai Katsumoto in the film, *The Last Samurai*:

> The perfect blossom is a rare thing. You could spend your life looking for that, and it would not be a wasted life.

If you see or smell the aroma of a flower at any particular moment of thought, is it significant?

Do you keep seeing a certain type of flower? Do you keep finding flowers in the most random places? Don't disregard them. It could be a message.

This short story was sent to me by my cousin Andria, who read this book before it was officially published.

Andria's Story (in Her Own Words)

Andrew, this is really not made up. This morning my mum picked a rose from her garden and put it in a vase. A little later, there was glitter all over it. We all had pink roses with glitter on them for my grandmother's funeral.

The following was from a friend of mine named Lisa after she read the first edition of this book:

Lisa's Story (in Her Own Words)

I never thought of things being signs before. An incident that happens a lot to me is when I take flowers to the cemetery for my dad, one head always falls off. I believe he always wants me to have that one for myself.

Another gift from above are petals from flowers left in strange places for you to see. I regularly see one single petal somewhere totally random, like the boot of my car. Or lots of them spread out around me when I'm anxious or worried about something. Another friend of mine recently explained how his friend talked about the formation of petals in a lake and how he believed they were a present to him from the universe.

As I conclude this chapter, there's a lady standing at the counter of the coffee shop, carrying a bunch of flowers, and the time is 1.11 p.m. You really can't write this stuff.

Butterflies

Butterflies are amazing creatures, heaven sent, some people believe. What other creature in the world transforms itself from a caterpillar to a beautiful, and often colourful, butterfly?

Many people talk about butterflies and their significance to heaven or a loved one. Not so long ago, I saw a TV interview with a woman who saw yellow butterflies quite often after her daughter had passed away. Her daughter always loved the colour yellow. For the mother, this was a comforting sign, a message from her daughter that she was alright and safe in heaven.

Another similar but astonishing story happened to a friend of a friend after her daughter was tragically killed in a car accident. A beautiful green hairstreak butterfly flew into her room and stayed there all night. A few days later, after the funeral, the butterfly came back and settled on the top of the ashes container and remained there for a while. Sometime after that, a post memory appeared on Facebook of her daughter holding a butterfly in her hand when she was aged just five. The mother took comfort from this that there is life after death.

When I was writing the first edition of this book, I kept seeing white butterflies and always when I was thinking of something significant.

By the way, you don't have to see real butterflies for them to be signs. They could be pictures of butterflies on books, t-shirts, wallpaper, greeting cards, and so on.

It's also believed that seeing different colour butterflies have a specific meaning, whether it's a real butterfly or a picture of one.

I must add, I was in two minds whether to include the following meanings of butterfly colours. The idea came to me whilst in meditation one day during the third edition edit. However, as per usual, the universe got my attention just a few days after I wrote it.

Firstly, I was looking for a birthday card for a spiritual friend of mine when the most amazing card popped out at me. It was of a multicoloured butterfly on a white background. I bought it for her.

Secondly, I can't remember exactly where I was, or who it was, but someone was holding a greeting card with lots of gold butterflies on it. I chuckled to myself and decided to include the following in the book.

Here are the meanings:

White: Be yourself. You don't have to dress to impress or wear a mask. If someone doesn't like you for being you, perhaps it's time to move on.

Yellow: Things happen for a good reason. Trust the process, even if it doesn't seem to be working out as you hoped it would.

Green: Your dear departed loved ones are with you. Know they are sending you a sign from beyond the grave to let you know everything is okay.

Brown: Someone special is thinking about you. You are loved more than you know. You are worth it, and people appreciate you.

Orange: You are a spiritual person. Don't worry about offending people with your beliefs, and don't try to convince people. Not everyone will agree with you, and that's okay. Meditate and talk to your angels.

Pink: Love yourself. Your angels are sending you love and support. Make sure any thoughts you have about yourself are good. Replace negative with positive. You are attracting love.

Red: You have a good heart. Everything you do is for a good reason. Don't doubt that feeling in your heart. Listen to your heart for answers.

Gold: Abundance. Riches are coming your way. You are attracting money. Think positively about money. A project you're working on is going to be a success. Stick with it.

: Happiness and joy. You deserve to be happy and are making decisions that will allow that to happen. Saying no is not always a bad thing. Stop trying to please everyone.

Grey: Creativity. You are being urged to do more with your creative side, whether it be to write, draw, paint, sing, dance, act, and so on. Have you been talking yourself out of doing what you love? Now's the time to release the beast.

Black: Clear conscience. Stop worrying about things that happened, and live in the present. You made mistakes but must move forward now. Don't dwell on the past. We all make mistakes. Forgive yourself.

Coincidences

How often have you encountered something that you were quick to explain as coincidence? When, for instance, you were thinking about calling someone on your mobile, and they call you?

Or you travel to a country thousands of miles away, only to see someone from your own hometown.

Is it really coincidence or the universe speaking to us again? Reminding us of its almighty power. Telling us we shouldn't ignore it, we should believe in miracles.

The amazing true story of Annabel Beam could all too easily be explained as coincidence.

Annabel's story was documented in a book by her mother, Christy Beam, and made into a film of the same name, *Miracles from Heaven*. If you haven't seen this film, please don't read the rest of this chapter until you have because it contains a spoiler. And it's a big one too.

So hopefully you've now seen the movie. Great. Read on.

Annabel Beam fell head first thirty feet into a hollow tree, and when firemen got her out four hours later, there was no serious injury to her at all. Doctors were amazed. Even more amazing, she was cured of an intestinal disorder she had suffered from since the age of five.

Annabel said she went to heaven and spoke to Jesus. He told her she would go back and be healed. In the movie, Dr Nurko explained that when she fell, her central nervous system may have been regenerated, like her software had been reset. He said doctors used the term spontaneous remission to explain that which cannot be explained. And when Christy asked if she had been cured, he claimed there was no cure for Annabel's condition.

Is this coincidence?

The message is to think twice when a coincidence happens to you. What is the universe trying to tell you? Why has this situation happened so miraculously? There could be a reason for it.

Leaves

Leaves, like flower petals, have a way of telling us we are being looked after.

I remember telling a friend of mine, "I'm seeing leaves falling directly in front of me all the time."

She replied, "Well, that might have something to do with autumn."

We laughed, but the truth is, one single leaf would fall directly in front of my path either while driving or walking. Regularly.

Recently, I have seen single, dry leaves appearing regularly in front of me, in odd places, like on the carpet in my bedroom, in the boot of my car, blowing past me while driving, or in a random box. I almost always step out of the house in the morning and see a different one waiting for me on the doorstep.

Of course, leaves get everywhere in autumn, but it's becoming aware of whether it's a sign or just the season. My belief is, everything is a sign, and if you are open to it, then the universe will show you that sign.

When I went to Psychicmaiden for a reading while writing this book, she told me a lot of things that were significant. Rhian didn't know I was working on this book back then, and before leaving, I asked to use the bathroom. As I stepped out, there on the carpeted floor was a single dry leaf. How did it get there?

I have taken endless pictures of random leaves over the years, and you can see them on the Instagram account.

Feathers

Feather signs are popular and probably the most well-known form of spiritual messages.

Just before I wrote the first edition of this book, I mentioned to a friend of mine that I was seeing feathers everywhere. On the floor, in my car, falling from the sky, on television adverts, in the clouds, and so on. I told her I was sure they were messages from above, and I think she thought I was crazy.

Then a few days later, we were at work when she came into my office, looking a little surprised.

"You will never guess what just happened," she said.

"No, what?" I asked.

"Well," she went on, "I was on the phone to a friend of mine who is having a hard time, whilst looking out of the second-floor window, when this tiny white feather fell so delicately from the sky in front of me."

"Never," I exclaimed with a tiny smirk on my face.

"I know," she said. "And I told my friend everything will all be okay."

It's incidents like these that have persuaded me to write this book. So that the millions (or even billions) of unsuspecting people out there can also begin to receive messages of hope in their lives.

Feathers appear to us when we are trying to make decisions we're not sure about or when a loved one passes over. They are assurances to let us know our loved one is in a good place, and they are happy.

When my sister's partner's mother passed away a few years ago, a feather appeared on his doorstep out of nowhere and remained lodged in the corner for months. Was this a message?

Feathers can be seen everywhere, and certain colours are believed to be significant. Here's what some experts say:

White: Faith and protection. An angel is telling you that a loved one is safe in heaven.

Pink: Your angels love you unconditionally.

Purple: Spiritual. Your angels are telling you to connect with your higher purpose.

Red: Represents courage, strength, passion, and good fortune. Loved ones in heaven are well.

Yellow: Be cheerful, smile, and have fun.

Green: Prosperity and growth. It's lucky to find a green feather.

Blue: Peaceful and calming. Also, a sign to listen.

Grey: Certain things may not be so straightforward.

Black: You are protected by your angels.

Brown: Symbolises home and grounding. Your home life will see positivity soon.

Orange: Ideas and opportunities are approved by your angels. Stay positive to attract success.

As you already know, I teach karate, and around twelve years ago, when I opened a new after-school club, I had around twenty children join. One of those children was a five-year-old girl named Angel, and her coat literally had white feathers all over it. I remember it being another difficult time in my life and knowing that this was a nice little sign from the angels.

Coins

The one thing I've struggled with all my life is low self-esteem. As a result, I was never any good at the dating game or relationships. This has been an ongoing and difficult theme in my life; whether it's down to shear bad luck or that I'm too fussy, I've never quite managed to find the woman of my dreams.

Anyway, some years ago, when I felt worthless and was going through a hard time wondering if I would ever find love, I remember seeing shiny one-pence pieces everywhere. I knew they were a spiritual sign, but I just needed to know exactly what was being communicated to me. I often begged for an answer. Now I believe they were shown to me as reassurance that things would get better, which they did. I also began to notice shiny five-pence pieces at significant times of doubt.

In the Greek tradition, we bake (actually, it's my mum who does the baking) a sponge cake for New Year's Day with a coin hidden somewhere inside. Whoever finds the coin, it's said that they will have a lucky year.

Coins are often tossed into ponds and lakes by people who want their wishes to come true.

So why are coins thought to be a spiritual sign? I mean, it's money, and money is supposed to be the root of all evil, right?

I decided to do some research and found this interesting story from the Bible. It's called the Parable of the Lost Coin, from Luke 15:8–10:

> There was a woman who owned ten coins, each one precious to her. She would take time to clean and shine them often. One day, she noticed that one had gone missing.
>
> Desperate to find it, she searched every nook and cranny of the house. She cleaned and swept until she eventually found the coin and rejoiced.

Why is this story relevant? God (or the universe) thinks of us just as the woman did the coin. We are precious to Him, and He will not let any of us get lost. That's why Jesus originally told the story to the nonbelievers, to explain that they were also precious to God.

And I believe (and it's just my opinion) that when we find coins, it is God letting us know we are precious to Him, and He's just letting us know. He is there for us. He is assuring us that we are not alone.

If you're finding coins everywhere, it's the universe telling you that whatever is happening in your life, if you are lost, you are struggling, or you feel alone, you're not. The universe is with you.

If you see coins of certain values, perhaps use the numbers guide above. For instance, when I was finding five-pence pieces everywhere years ago, could it have been God telling me to have strength and courage? I wish I had this guidebook back then.

Clouds

If in doubt, look up. You will often see messages in the sky from clouds.

In 2002, I had a cat named Shandy who was nineteen years old. One day when I was at work, my father phoned to let me know Shandy had died; he been a part of my life for nineteen years, so I was understandably upset.

Tearfully, I told the lads at work, and as we stood outside having coffee that morning, I looked up to see this almighty paw in the clouds. I pointed it out, and one of them agreed with what I was thinking.

"It's a sign," he said. "She's up there."

Not so long ago, my friends Graham and Claire lost their dearly beloved Yorkshire/Jack Russell terrier named Cassie. On that very same day, at sunset, they saw a cloud on the horizon that closely resembled Cassie, and they were convinced it was a message to let them know she was okay. They kindly shared a photo they took, and you can find it at the Instagram page and also at our Facebook page.

In clouds, you can often see various shapes and patterns such as faces, angels, feathers, animals, heart shapes, countries, and so much more.

Keep your eyes open.

Heart Shapes

Hearts can be seen everywhere: on sweaters, t-shirts, television, book covers, greeting cards, mugs, and trademarks; in coffee cups; in the clouds; on the floor. There is no end to this, and if you see them, just remember, love is all around you, and maybe you need to spread the love too.

Rhonda Byrne deals beautifully with love in her book, *The Power*. And her main message is to love, no matter what. Because love is healing, love is attracting, love is powerful and love is the cause of everything positive and good.

In her book, she talks about sending love out to everyone and to the world, but also to yourself. Many people forget to love themselves because they think it's selfish or egotistical. Remember the old but wise saying, "If you cannot love yourself, then how can you love another?"

Seeing hearts is a reminder to send love out and to love yourself.

Here are a few lovely quotes from Byrne's book:

Love, because when you love you are using the greatest power in the universe.

You have an unlimited ability to think and talk about what you love, and so you have an unlimited ability to bring everything good in life to you!

Everything you want to be, do or have comes from love.

Natural Sounds

Sounds from our natural surroundings, like birds tweeting, are always going to offer us comfort, and the more in tune we are with nature, the more we will hear and appreciate this amazing world we live in.

I recommend sitting in total silence with your window open occasionally, to hear these beautiful sounds. It's music to the ears. Morning is best.

Other natural sounds can be the bark of a dog, the miaow of a cat, the wind blowing through the trees, children laughing, rain falling, ocean waves lapping on shore, cows mooing, and sheep baa-ing.

This is like the radio station of the universe transmitting to us, letting us know we are not alone. Yet so many people miss this.

If you ever find yourself alone and feeling lonely, just take time to listen. God is sure to send you company.

High-Pitched Sounds

This is something I was totally unaware of until I read Kyle Gray's book, *Raise Your Vibration*. Kyle explains that high-pitched sounds are a download of divine guidance from the universe, like something that will be revealed to us in due course.

He also makes an interesting point that we are like huge radios tuned in to receive messages from heaven. However, our frequencies are not always perfectly tuned but can still receive certain channels. Much like a radio.

I have always had a keen interest in the law of attraction and having read many books on the subject, including *The Secret* by Rhonda Byrne. I have come to believe we are just like TV aerials. We, as human beings, are set to receive signals just like a TV that plays out on the screen as a movie or show. If our aerial (mind) is not perfectly set, our movie (life) will be distorted (attract less of what we want) or won't show at all.

If you're as old as me, you may remember the days when downloading a game onto a Spectrum ZX80? We would link up one of those flat tape recorders and press play. Then there was this high-pitched screeching sound that went on for what seemed like ages, but was actually around five minutes. We would then be able to play a game like Manic Miner on the screen.

This happens to me regularly, especially at significant moments of thought or decisions. High-pitched sounds ring out in either my left or right ear for a few seconds, sometimes quite intense. I believe the universe is guiding me with information I need to move forward. So when it happens, I thank God and ask to be enlightened. Either that or pray there's nothing seriously wrong with me.

My advice is, become an aerial, so to speak, that sends out positive energy to the universe, which in turn attracts positive events. Think of yourself as one of the billions of different frequencies being transmitted all over the world (and universe), receiving what you want and not what you don't want. Put simply, think only positive thoughts.

There's more on the law of attraction later in the book.

Songs

Songs have a way of getting our attention. Have you ever been worried about something, only to hear a song that puts your mind at rest? Maybe the lyrics spoke directly to you or the song was significant in some way?

Back when I was going through the worst time of my life, after having my first panic attack, I found it hard to go out. I was too worried I'd have a panic attack again, which I usually did. We had a family trip planned to Disney World, and the idea of being stuck in an aeroplane for nine hours scared the hell out of me. I had a choice to make: go or stay home?

Of course, there was no way I was staying home because going to Florida was a dream come true. I was a massive fan of the movies, and there was no way I was missing out on trips to places like MGM and Universal Studios. So, with permission to carry my Chinese health balls onto the plane, I decided to go.

When we got there, waiting in long queues for attractions wasn't easy, especially when there's a constant lump in your throat. But I managed, with the help of my cousin's jokes, mainly about me being a nervous wreck. I mentioned to my sister that I couldn't cope for two weeks like this and wanted to go home.

That was until I started to hear the song "Hero" by Mariah Carey. It was constantly playing on the radio, and I was sure it was a message from God. The words gave me a renewed strength to look into my heart; to not be afraid, and to cast all my fears aside. Almost every word seemed to be aimed at me.

Needless to say, I stayed and after a difficult first week, I thoroughly enjoyed the second.

Has a song spoken to you recently?

Smells

Sometimes, messages come in the form of smells, like the myrrh scent I mentioned earlier, church smells, candles, or incense sticks.

One evening, after my karate classes, I was driving home when this smoky smell seemed to come from outside. It was like a church smell. I thought nothing of it and kept driving, but a mile down the road, it came into my car again. I thought it must be coming from outside, so I opened my window, expecting to smell smoke. Nothing.

Was it a sign? Maybe. I challenged it: *If that's a sign, let me smell it once again*. My heart skipped a beat when, a little later down the road, the same smell seeped into my car. I couldn't believe it.

I'm still not certain if this smoky smell was a sign, but over the years, I have smelt similar scents out of nowhere.

Recently, I attended a psychic medium event in my hometown. A woman named Nataly spoke to one of the audience members about her best friend, who had recently passed away. Sarah, the lady in the audience, mentioned a cigarette smell she just couldn't get rid of; she even went to the doctor. She didn't smoke, but her best friend did. According to Nataly, Sarah's best friend had been giving her a sign that she was okay.

A Light Touch

I didn't notice this until I began to meditate daily. It feels as though I'm being touched very lightly with a feather, usually on my face. I also feel warm sensations on various parts of my body. In fact, as I write this, I have this feeling of something pressing its thumb on the top of my head, as though saying, "Come on, get a move on. You need to finish this book."

In Lorna Byrne's enlightening autobiography, *Angels in My Hair*, she explains how angels would ruffle her hair; this began when she was a young girl. And in her book, *Angels at My Fingertips*, Lorna explains how you can touch your angel with your hands.

This isn't a common sign but if you tune into the spirit world, you'll most likely become aware of it too.

You may feel light touches on your face and hands, get a sudden warm feeling on your skin like a heat pad being placed on it, feel a tingling sensation, or have a sudden need to itch.

It's a case of becoming aware of it and thanking your angels for letting you know they are with you. Have faith.

Coffee Cups

You may not know this, but I'm Greek Cypriot, and being Greek Cypriot means I love my Greek coffee. I usually make time for it with my parents once a day.

Greek coffee, same as Turkish, is boiled in a small pot and poured into a small cup, like espresso. However, the coffee grounds don't dissolve. Instead, they sit at the bottom of the cup, and people stop drinking the moment they start to feel it on their tongue.

When a Greek coffee is initially poured, some of the coffee grounds create a thin layer of foam on the top (known as *kaimaki*). It often creates shapes like hearts, faces, bubbles, angels, and so much more. Some psychics can read your fortune from your cup once you've drank it because it leaves shapes around the inside of the cup.

I believe signs and messages are often found in Greek coffee, so the next time you have one, take a close look.

One Sunday morning in March 2019, I had a Facebook memory pop up showing me a Greek coffee I drank in 2013. When I went into my memories to have a look at other memories on this day, another memory of a Greek coffee popped up, posted in 2014. The shape made from that coffee foam was two eyes and a mouth smiling. It was uncanny.

At that moment, I pointed it out to my parents, and we decided to have a cup.

My mother made the coffee and brought it in a tray to myself and my father in the lounge. They chose their coffee and left me with one. Unbelievably, my coffee had an almost identical face to the one seen in 2014. We were amazed.

You can see this comparison on the Instagram page @TheSecretSignsBook.

In fact, that was the same week I was concerned about some blood tests and was being bombarded with similar signs of comfort. Lo and behold, everything turned out to be alright.

Signs That May Go Unnoticed

Have you ever been working on your laptop, tablet, or other device when it froze or crashed? Has your Wi-Fi dropped out for no apparent reason? Isn't that frustrating?

How do you react? Do you try your best to get it working, wait patiently for it to right itself, or throw your tablet across the room in anger?

Have you ever thought that this may be a sign from above to put down the tablet and rethink what you were doing? Were you spending too much time on Facebook when it happened? Or sending a difficult email?

Instead of losing your cool, postpone whatever it was you were doing; if it's important, get back to it later. It could be God telling you something. Perhaps reconsider spending money on that expensive gadget from Amazon or commenting on your least favourite cousin's Facebook post.

I've found that the problem almost always fixes itself when I take a break and get back to it later. It saves me a lot of stress.

Smartphones also have this mysterious problem, so again, rethink what you were doing in the first place, and perhaps put it away.

Insects can also be a sign. For instance, a tiny fly landing on you repeatedly or an ant that won't go away. Don't kill it. It's a living creature and means no harm. Maybe it has come to tell you something.

Some weeks ago, whilst karate training in one of the local community halls, there were no less than sixteen daddy long legs in the room with us. But the eeriest part about it was, they didn't move at all for the three hours we were there. They just sat on the walls, surrounding us like a pack of wolves. Days later, someone posted on one my Facebook groups that crane flies are extremely spiritual. Wow! Even I didn't know that.

Names of people we meet could be messages from God. Angel, for instance. Or names such as Faith, Joy, Gabriel (Archangel), or Theo (meaning God) may be trying to tell us something. Also, names that are personal to you. For example, you meet someone on the day you lose a dear relative who has the same name. This could be God letting you know your loved one is safe and well in heaven.

If you're religious, names popping up such as Joseph, Mary, Jesus, David, Eve, Grace, or Magdalene could also be significant to you.

In January 2007, when I embarked on two new businesses at the same time, karate and nutrition, two people had a significant role in the launch of these separate businesses. And they shared the same name: Angela. Both called me on the same day, and had they not, I might be living a very different life today. It gets even spookier because one of them had a significant surname too. I cannot share this for privacy reasons but because of this wonderful lady, my karate career really took off.

You may notice subtle messages on notice boards of churches, shops, or community centres. One day, when I was having a bad day and questioning everything, I noticed a piece of paper pinned to a notice board in a community hall. It said something like, "Do Not Try to Understand God, Just Trust."

Other signs you may be unaware of are seeing smoke from the corner of your eye, hearing bells ringing, hearing beautiful heavenly music, seeing newspaper headlines, or hearing your name being called when no one is there.

A stranger smiling at you on the street could also be a sign. We human beings are energy, and we act on energy from our universe or angels, who may be sending us to do something in particular. For instance, I wasn't planning to write this book. It kind of just happened. It came about because of my experiences, and I felt compelled to help others. So when someone out of the blue smiles at you in public, and you feel so much better for it, this could be a sign from God too. This has happened to me many times.

Rainbows also have a way of coming out just in time to reassure us. When Queen Elizabeth II passed away on Thursday, 8 September 2022, the most magnificent double rainbow appeared over Buckingham Palace just before her death was announced. Double rainbows are considered quite rare.

Be Faithful

When I was a teenager, everything seemed to be a struggle. I could never relax and truly enjoy myself, always worrying about something. Money was a big problem back then, but so was my well-being. I used to get ill and tired a lot, and couldn't train as hard (and as often) as I wanted to. Going out was a chore most of the time, and Christmas, well, Christmas just brought me more money problems.

I worried about what other people thought about me and couldn't be myself. I chose the wrong path in university to please others and ended up working in an industry that really wasn't for me.

Fear stopped me from pursuing most of my dreams. I wanted to be a writer, filmmaker, drummer, and DJ. And although I had the opportunity to do all of those things, I talked my way out of them every time.

I'm still not completely fear-free; however, I am living life with my foot off the brakes now. The last fifteen years have been the best time of my life, and a lot has to do with becoming more faithful, knowing we're not here to suffer but to achieve everything we desire and to trust that the universe has our back.

I recently asked a lot of questions of the universe with regards to achieving goals, self-healing, happiness, love, the meaning life, our purpose, my purpose, and much more. I believe I've received answers through meditation, dreams, films, audio books, books, eavesdropping, notice boards, and newspaper headlines, to name but a few. I truly believe if we just stop, listen, have complete faith, and open our mind, the universe speaks back.

Here is an example of asking questions and receiving answers:

While meditating, I recently asked a lot about illness and if we (humans) are capable of self-healing. It's a question I've repeatedly asked for a while now, and I believe, my asking has led to many answers. Here are some of the numerous answers I received, which I highly recommend you look into:

1) Deepak Chopra's Audible *The Ultimate Deepak Chopra Collection*
2) *Heal,* a movie available on Netflix.
3) Ayurveda, which is closely linked to yoga
4) *Applying the 10 Secrets for Success and Inner Peace* by Dr Wayne W. Dyer and available only on Audible.
5) *A Course in Miracles* by Helen Schucman (book and audio book)

I am no more special than anyone else; I'm convinced, if you have true faith and ask questions, you too will receive answers.

Divine Intervention

I believe God has a way of getting our attention. Whether through the signs already mentioned or by miracles that happen every day, throughout the world.

Albert Einstein was famous for saying, "There are only two ways to live your life. One is as though nothing is a miracle. The other is as though everything is a miracle."

Throughout the early years of my life, I lived as though nothing was a miracle, often blaming God for everything, for not giving me what I thought I deserved. I even remember a time when I lost my faith completely. "Why should I believe?" I challenged Him. "You've never given me what I want. I'm always the unlucky one. I never get the girl. I never get the money. I never get the success."

I grew up with a negative attitude, and when great things happened, which was quite often, I never noticed them. I was too busy wallowing in my own sorrow. I had debts coming out of my ears, went from job to job wishing I was doing something else, and always seemed to say the wrong things to people.

Looking back, I realise I have lived a blessed life, with a beautiful family and some amazing friends. In fact, I've been lucky. No, actually, I've been very lucky. I can remember three occasions when I could have died but for what I believe was a divine intervention.

Let's look at them:

The first occasion was when I was around nine years old. My parents used to own a fish and chip shop in Barry, South Wales. When they finished at night, they often went to see some friends at their restaurant in Barry Island.

One particular evening, I was with them quite late, and by the time they reached their destination, I was fast asleep in the back seat. My dad parked the car outside the popular restaurant where they could see it, and they were about to go in without me. It sounds bad, but they intended to keep a close eye on the locked car.

I woke up at the last moment and begged to come in with them. My mum told me it would be okay and to stay asleep in the car, but I kept begging. So they took me in with them, and I slept on her lap while she talked and drank coffee (or was it a glass of wine, I can't quite remember).

About fifteen or twenty minutes later, a drunk driver came speeding down the long road leading to the restaurant, lost control of his car, and crashed into the back of my dad's car. He struck our car so hard, it hit the van parked in front, which hit the car in front of it. The drunk man got out and ran off, but they caught him some time later.

I often wonder what would have happened to me that evening had I been in the car. But what I wonder most of the time is why I was so adamant to get out of the car. In the past, I would have stayed there and slept. Miracle 1.

Sometime after that, while I was still in primary school, the next divine intervention took place. It was lunchtime, and I left my parents' chip shop to walk the short distance to the school. As I crossed the busy road to go to the sweet shop, I couldn't have looked properly. I heard a car horn and turned to my left to see a car coming straight at me.

I can remember it clearly because the car horn seemed to go on forever, and I was paralysed with the fear. In fact, I remember watching safety advice adverts on television about crossing the road, and it showed kids stopping in the middle and looking at the car. I would often say, "As if they would stop in the middle of the road." Well, that's exactly what I did.

The driver, a young man wearing tinted sunglasses, right out of the late 1970s, slammed on his brakes and screeched to a halt, centimetres away from my legs. I was in shock. The next thing I clearly remember was the driver breathing the biggest sigh of relief.

When I eventually came to and got out of the road, I leant into his passenger-side window, which was open, to say, "I'm sorry," in the most weakest of ways. He was lost for words. Miracle 2.

The third incident happened to me many years later when I was driving. It was a cold, rainy morning, and my brother needed a lift to work in Cardiff. I was a little annoyed because I had plans that morning, and it would make me late.

I dropped him off and drove around to some lights which led onto Cowbridge Road, an extremely busy main road. Usually, I would just drive off when the green lights showed, but something stopped me from doing so. I don't quite know what.

Instead, I crept slowly towards the main road with my car and looked right to make sure cars had stopped. In fact, they hadn't, and a large blue van whizzed past me just inches away. He had to swerve slightly outwards to miss me, and I dread to think what would have happened if I had just driven forward without caution. Miracle 3.

For me, these were definite moments of divine intervention which I am now truly grateful for.

What divine interventions have occurred in your life? Please feel free to email me on thesecretsigns@hotmail.com

Sporting Interventions

I'm a massive fan of sports, but none more so than true stories of individuals and teams winning through adversity. I also love a great underdog success story.

What has this got to do with signs, you may ask?

My belief is that the almighty universe rewards those who believe, work hard, and never quit, regardless of what they want to achieve. More so, I believe teams that work in true harmony with each other, each one trusting the other, become the champions they so desire eventually.

And each true story of success that exists, past or present, serves as a reminder to us that whatever we desire in life, we can achieve it.

I've chosen three amazing sporting achievements as examples of this. All are from the year 2019; I picked these because they're fresh in my mind.

Don't get me wrong; these teams worked hard for their successes. Because of their unbelievable, consistent hard work, I believe something helped them over the line. Funny enough, two of the examples are from the football Champions League.

The UEFA Champions League, 2018-2019

The whole tournament was a topsy-turvy one, with Ajax beating some of the best in the world, and Tottenham Hotspurs progressing through the group stages after a very poor start against Inter Milan, Barcelona, and PSV Eindhoven.

But what happened in both semifinals was one of the most memorable I will ever see and have ever seen in football, full stop.

First of all, there was Liverpool's astonishing comeback from 3-0 down (in the first leg) against arguably the best in the world, Barcelona, to win 4-3 (in the second leg). No one would have bet on this (well, probably one or two did).

And the very next day, Spurs came back from 3-0 down to Ajax (over two legs) to draw 3-3. However, because Spurs had more away goals, they won on away goals rule. And it was done on the very last kick of the game. If fact, it was precisely one second after the allotted injury time. Had they not scored, Ajax were going through.

As one commentator said, "Spurs rode their luck throughout the tournament," and in the game before the Ajax semifinals, Spurs went through in the very last minutes of the game, again on the away goals rule, when Manchester City's goal was ruled offside thanks to the all-new Video Assistant Referee (VAR).

The Cricket World Cup, 2019

I'm not a cricket fan, but when England got through to the finals of the world cup in 2019, I decided I would watch it. Actually, I had the TV on the channel and watched what I could throughout the day whilst doing some work. I'll be honest, I'm not the type of person to sit down and watch hours and hours of television, regardless of what's on.

But as the game drew to a close, I couldn't help but become more engrossed. It was a close affair, and England somehow won it through some unbelievable individual performances and one or two twists of fate (maybe even three or four).

One of those amazing twists was when the ball was thrown from a distance to the man by the wickets, but it hit Ben Stokes's bat as he dived for home. It deflected the ball, and they had to retrieve it again.

There's no way I can describe the game because I don't even know the rules, so I've added the following report from the Telegraph Online, dated 15 July 2019.

It seemed as though nothing could separate them from New Zealand, with the sides battling to an unprecedented tie, both sides locked on 241 after 100 overs of nerve-shredding tension that cast Ben Stokes as the home side's hero of the hour.

That paved the way for a super over, a six-ball shoot-out that had only occurred 11 times in international history and never before in an ODI.

Incredibly, the teams went blow-for-blow once again, Stokes and Jos Buttler hitting 15 off Trent Boult before Jofra Archer conceded 14 off his first five deliveries.

The Barbados-born bowler, the least experienced player on either side, held his nerve as Martin Guptill forced the ball into the off-side and came back for a second that would have taken the trophy.

Enter Jason Roy, who picked up cleanly despite unimaginable pressure and hurled a flat, decisive throw towards Buttler, who scattered the stumps as Guptill scrambled.

Tied once again, England triumphed on account of boundaries scored in the original 50-over match, a technocratic decider in a contest that proved impossible to settle any other way.

In the end England's 22 fours and two sixes proved the difference, besting the Black Caps' tally of 14 and two but they are just numbers, and do scant justice to the emotional, occasionally controversial and endlessly replayable events that played out on this famous ground.

Rarely has the tension at this storied stadium reached such emphatic peaks and rarely has a winning team celebrated with such gusto, the game and all the prizes that go with it having seemingly disappeared from their grasp on several occasions.

I love what *A Course in Miracles* says about miracles: "Miracles are natural, when they do not happen, something is wrong."

Again, I'm not at all trying to say any of the above achievements were miracles, and I do not attempt to disregard their performances. Totally the opposite. From hard work, belief, consistency, faith, and never giving up, comes success. And that's what I love about stories.

Signs whilst You Sleep

We all have dreams. Some we remember, most we don't. But have you ever stopped to ask yourself whether dreams are messages from God?

So many times over the years, I've woken up feeling great because of a dream. It may have been because I met my soul mate and we hugged, or I saw my late cat, Shandy, who passed away twenty years ago, and we played in the garden, or it may have been a dream of flying.

I've even had the odd dream come true. Such as becoming a black belt or earning a royalty cheque with my nutrition business. Like many others, I've dreamt of late relatives who popped in to say hello. I've also dreamt of spiritual beings such as the Virgin Mary. Not so long ago, she came to me as a giant and placed her hand on my head, explaining that she was healing me. One Christmas morning, I dreamt of the most beautiful UFO (similar to the one in the movie *Close Encounters*) hovering above my house. It felt so powerful, as though the UFO symbolised Jesus coming down to earth.

As mentioned earlier, I began to question numerous things in life. Many of those questions were to do with our health because of the corona virus outbreak. For instance, why do we get sick? Or how can we heal ourselves naturally? Whilst most of the answers came to me in physical form by way of books, videos, articles, movies, and blogs, one of the answers came to me while I slept.

One night in April 2020, I dreamt I was making a movie, and someone in the dream told me the name of the movie. It was *Faith Heals*. I firmly believe it was a message from above confirming what I already believe to be true: that we humans are far more capable of healing than we give credit.

I have come to believe that if we ask questions, we receive some of those answers through our dreams.

Law of Attraction

When I wrote the first two editions of this book, I never made the connection between the law of attraction and the signs. Although I'm a big believer of the law of attraction and have read many books on the subject, it wasn't until a friend of mine explained that noticing signs means the universe is letting us know we're on the right track.

Jo Cantle, who is a manifesting coach, explained that the universe lets us know through treble and multiple numbers (and other obvious signs) that it supports us and encourages us to have faith.

The following true story of how Jo's kittens were attracted into her life is a beautiful example of accepting and trusting the process.

My Law of Attraction Kitties, by Jo Cantle

Back in August 2020, we had to make the heartbreaking decision to euthanise our seventeen-year-old cat, Fynn. Her kidney problems had worsened in the space of a week, and eventually we had to let her go. Easing the suffering of a beloved pet is personally painful but necessary. It never gets easier. Back then, we were still in a partial COVID lockdown—long hours confined to a house that felt so quiet without her spirit and energy. We knew we would eventually get more cats (my husband and I adore cats and have always had them), but we couldn't face the idea while we were still grieving.

By September 2020, I was struggling terribly—missing my girl and longing to bring more cats into our home again. My husband just didn't feel ready, and I wanted to respect his feelings; however, I was inspired to visit the RSPCA rescue pages occasionally, just to see if "my" cats were there.

For a few weeks, I looked and felt the pull, but I knew that the cats I'd seen were not my cats. I had already decided I wanted to get a pair of kittens: sisters, one black (like our Fynn had been) and one tuxedo, because I had always liked the look of them.

I felt a yearning to bring new furry family members into our home, and also, within that, there was a lot of resistance (I'm a Law of Attraction Life Coach, so I knew I was creating my own blocks). One day, I just let go; I surrendered the longing.

I just said, "I'm letting go, God. I know the right cats will come into my life when they're ready."

The next day, I was at work and felt that familiar pull to look on the RSPCA website for the latest updates. I spotted a male tuxedo cat called Picasso; despite knowing I wanted two females, I was open to any possibility. Perhaps I could get two cats, who were not related, but I could adopt both at the same time.

I liked the idea of Picasso; he was a year old, and he looked a cheeky chap, so I decided to fill in an adoption form. However, I couldn't find an email address for the RSPCA site where he was, just a phone number. So I called.

Dawn, the lady on the end of the phone, said, "Oh, I'm sorry; Picasso has been adopted. I've not had a chance to update the website. What are you looking for?"

I told her my ideal request.

Dawn listened and then replied, "Well, I've got two pairs of kittens coming in today, only eight weeks. I'll send you over their photos. One pair of girls, one pair of boys."

Seconds later, I received the first photo of two adorable kittens: one black, one tuxedo. I knew these were the ones; I raced upstairs to see my husband and show him. What I hadn't spotted was that Dawn had written underneath, "This is the male pair."

My husband read it, handed it back to me, and said, "They're not girls. That's not what you said you wanted."

The other photo came through. Two tortoiseshell females; gorgeous, but I knew, somehow, that those first kittens were mine.

I messaged back immediately to request a visit to see them; due to lockdown restrictions, it was a week later. I couldn't wait. I knew that once I spent time with them, the deal would be done. The following week, we met Dawn at the shelter.

She said, "I'll leave you to get to know them."

We then spent forty-five minutes trying to catch the two scamps, as they raced around the holding pens. It was safe to say, it was love at first sight; I didn't care if they were boys. These were our cats.

Dawn returned. I just said, "They're adorable," to which she replied, "Oh, you like the sisters, then."

I was confused. "But you said these were boys?"

She replied, "Sorry, I got confused because we had the two sets arrive on the same day. No, these are definitely girls."

At which point, I just wept. I knew that the universe had orchestrated exactly what I had wanted, and these were our kittens.

Two abandoned feral kittens found sheltering under a shed, along with a third sibling adopted by the people who rescued them. They were incredibly nervous and wary, but I'm a strong believer that every animal just needs patience, love, and understanding, of which we have an inexhaustible supply. They required a further four weeks of care at the shelter: medical checks, monitoring, and essential vaccinations, before we could adopt. On 18 November 2020, we welcomed Luna and Magic into our home.

Now, two years on, we are blessed with two beautiful, affectionate, funny, and cheeky furballs. I am so grateful how the universe fulfilled our request. They give us so much love and joy.

It's almost coincidental, or once again, the universe doing her magic that I have a similar story to Jo's in that Maia, my cat, came along after another bout of anxiety in 2021. I kept saying I wanted a cat to help take my mind off negative thoughts, but I wasn't sure it was a wise decision for a number of reasons. Would I have time? Was I away too often? Could I handle the extra responsibility?

I hadn't had a cat for twenty years since Shandy, our beautiful white, black, and brown tabby. She passed away aged twenty, and I remember the hurt we experienced. This was another reason I wasn't sure.

However, I kept thinking about it and followed a few people who own cats on TikTok. One of those is a couple who have a brown tabby who's a real character. I've enjoyed many videos of this cat hugging, moaning, and meowing whilst, at the same time, wishing I had a cat like him.

Seven months later, my sister sent me a picture of an eight-month-old kitten owned by a separated couple who wanted their cat to go to a good home. I knew I wanted her straight away.

We picked her up, and fast-forward ten months, Maia is one of the best things that has ever happened to me. She is funny, moody, energetic, crazy, and playful; she is a cross between a Bengal and tabby, similar to the one I adore on TikTok.

If you're hoping for something to happen, set the intention by writing it down (or adding it to your vision board), and let the universe do the rest. During the time of waiting, weird things may happen, or you may see all sorts of signs, but don't try to make sense of anything. Just believe and trust the process.

In terms of money, many of us want to attract millions of pounds and be financially free, but so many of us have negative opinions of money.

Money is the root of all evil.

People with money are selfish.

Money doesn't grow on trees.

Money goes to money.

Over the years, I've read books on manifesting money and how to succeed as an entrepreneur, but it wasn't until I began to say positive words about money that it began to flow into my life. I'm not a millionaire, but things have drastically changed for me since I was in my late twenties.

My advice to anyone seeking money is to read good books on the subject, become an expert on your desired career path, learn how to handle money, and make a conscious decision to change your situation if you're not happy.

Here are a few tips to help manifest money:

1) If you see a penny or more on the floor, pick it up and say thank you for your find. Not picking up money of any value sends out the message you don't need it.
2) Fill up a jar of coins and put it somewhere you will see it daily. Say thank you for having money whenever you see the jar.
3) Visualise the good things you would do with money when you have it.
4) Say yes to opportunities that will potentially make you money, even if it's not much. Opportunities lead to opportunities.
5) Save 10 percent of your monthly income. If you can't afford that, save 5 percent or 1 percent. Something is better than nothing.
6) Do enter competitions to win money, but make sure you don't spend too much. My advice is to set a weekly limit on all gambling, such as £10. For instance, £4 on the lottery, £2 on the horses, £2 on a TV competition, and £2 on a scratch card. Play responsibly. Remember, you have to be in it to win it.
7) Some people believe that by giving, you will receive. Consider giving £10 a month (or whatever you can afford) to your favourite charity.
8) Say thank you for having a roof over your head every evening before you go to sleep.

Try this.

If you don't think you can manifest a million bucks, why not start small? Ask the universe for a shiny ten-pence piece, and wait for it to appear.

Not sure you can attract 10p? Take a leaf out of Jim Carrey's book. Before he was famous, he wrote himself a cheque for $10 million for acting services rendered and kept it in his wallet. Some years later, he found out he would be paid that exact amount for the film *Dumb and Dumber*.

Angels in Disguise

In recent years, so much has changed with regards to mental health and the rise of social media; it has become much more talked about. Consider the tragic death of Caroline Flack. Just weeks after she posted the following quote: "In a world where you can be anything, be kind," she took her own life. This led thousands of people to hashtag the words "be kind" on their own social media accounts.

When I suffered a nervous breakdown in November 1993, it quickly led to a deep depression no comedy or comedian could undo. I had low self-esteem and felt worthless. Christmas quickly arrived, and I had no desire to do any Christmas shopping, let alone wrap any presents. So I decided to go to a large supermarket and fill my trolley with all sorts of things like vodka, whiskey, deodorant gift sets, chocolates, and teddy bears. It was around seven or eight o'clock in the evening, and I remember the place being quiet.

Bear in mind, I was still struggling to keep calm when going out in public. I was anxious all the time and found it hard to breathe because of the tightness in my throat caused by the depression.

As I approached the checkout, I was nervous and felt like crying. I had no hope and wished I was dead, to put it bluntly.

When it was my turn, the girl behind the checkout began to talk to me; I remember her name was Laura and she was around eighteen years old. She made conversation, smiled, and asked how I was. Laura kept talking to me, asking who all the presents were for, joking and laughing as though I was one of her friends. In that moment, she made me feel so good about myself, like I wasn't invisible to the world, which is how I felt.

I can't quite remember the detail of our conversation or what I said back, but she made me feel happy for the first time in a while.

Laura changed my life that day with that one encounter. She gave me hope, and I left feeling stronger. Heaven sent, some would say.

The moral of the story, and of this chapter, is to be kind and be nice to each other. Ask people how they are, and listen. It doesn't take a lot to make someone happy, and you could save someone's life.

Be an angel in disguise, like Laura was for me, in a world where we go to a shop to buy something and often don't even get a hello.

And the funny thing is, as I finish this chapter, a friend I haven't heard from in a while has just messaged me to ask how I am. Thank you, Graham.

True Stories

I am inspired and given hope by the true stories of others overcoming challenges in their lives to achieve great things, to survive serious injury, or to heal themselves from illness. I believe stories like these are a message to us that we are capable of far more than we can even imagine. Below, I have included a few true stories that have inspired me.

The first story is about a friend of mine named Keith who, after a tragic accident, became paralysed from the neck down. Keith was told he would never walk again, yet he proved his doctors wrong.

Keith's Story (Written in His Own Words)

> In July 2018, I boarded a plane to Palma in Majorca, excited about a three-day stag do in Cala D'or. Little did I know would happen in the next twenty-four hours.
>
> Myself and a bunch of the lads were messing around in the pool, having fun, and I decided to dive in, just as I've done hundreds of times before. However, on this occasion, I got my angles wrong and knocked myself unconscious. At the same time, I broke two bones in my neck, and by the time they'd dragged me out, I'd stop breathing and had no pulse.
>
> If it hadn't have been for the quick thinking of a friend, who administered CPR on the side of the pool, I wouldn't be here writing this right now. I thank him every morning and every night.
>
> I was placed into an induced coma; my lungs were full of water, and I had swelling on my brain. My wife and dad flew over the next morning. When they arrived at the hospital, things were very uncertain. Would I wake up? If

I did, would I recognise them? Would I be able to communicate with them? These were all the unknowns, and they were told I would never walk again.

I remember coming to and looking up at my wife, my father, and my friend Jeff, who were at my bedside. I was thinking, *Hang on, they're not on the stag do; I must be dreaming.* So I closed my eyes before opening them again, and they were still there. My wife, Christina, told me I'd had an accident and broken my neck. Jeff said to me, "Blink once if you recognise us; blink twice if you don't." I blinked once.

So my new life began. I spent nearly three weeks in intensive care in Spain before I returned to the UK, to the spinal unit at the James Cook University Hospital in Middlesbrough. I was suffering from pneumonia, which was the first battle before I could even think about regaining any movement.

When I eventually came out of the high dependency unit, it was time to think about regaining some movement. I was still in a neck collar and could lift my arms a little; however, my hands had limited function. I couldn't move at all from the waist down, although I had slight feeling. If somebody touched me, I knew where. I would lie in bed trying to move my legs and toes, and nothing would happen. Then one day, I remember lying there trying to move my right foot and feeling a muscle flicker in my right shin. Nothing could be seen, but I was positive something was happening. The physios and doctors didn't agree. I'm sure they'd heard this hundreds of times from people in similar situations, desperate for some sort of sign.

I remember clearly, the day the consultant came in to do some further tests. Afterwards, he told me that if there was no improvement at the six-month mark, each month after that was a 50 percent drop in chances of recovery. Realising I only had two months to make things happen, I lost my enthusiasm and belief. I've always had a strong mind, but when the person you put your future in the hands of tells you something like that, you can only begin to waiver. I had a cry, and I had a wail.

Then I came to my senses. I wasn't letting any textbook talk ruin my chances of recovery. The phrase, "If it's to be, it's up to me," began to play in my mind. Challenge accepted. I'm not sure what it was, yet something was telling me never to give up. I was going try my hardest to make it.

My morning and evening ritual began. I would lie in bed, close my eyes, and imagine thoughts of movement going from my brain, down my neck, through my spinal cord, all the way down my back to each leg and to the tips of my toes. I would really engage in this. It was strange. I'd imagine it as a little blue light, my version of a nerve signal travelling from my brain downwards. Often, it would get stuck at my neck, the area that I damaged in the accident. I would work hard on this thought, working its way around the damaged area, finding any way possible to reroute and get through the damage. Like you're stuck in a traffic jam on a motorway and can take a side road through different windy roads before rejoining the motorway. That's what I would do. I have no idea how long this took. I was in a little world of my own. Sometimes it was minutes, sometimes it was a lot longer. I was lost in my own little world of remapping neural pathways. Morning and night without fail, this would be done.

The days were long and monotonous in hospital with very little to do, apart from watch television, and I can guarantee, I was the only person in that hospital ward working on their brain. I had to. I kept thinking of my family who depended on me. I was going to do my utmost to get back to normal.

Did it help? I have no idea. All I know is on 21 September 2018, seventy-eight days after being told I would never walk, I was lying in bed, looking at my right foot, thinking, *I'm going make that foot move.* And then I wiggled my left big toe. I was thinking, *Did I just do that?* I tried again, and it moved. This time, there was no doubt; the signals were getting through, and in that moment, I knew I would walk again.

I don't want to criticise the doctors and nurses, as they've been incredible and have helped with my recovery. My six months in hospital and all the follow-up physio sessions have been above and beyond. What more could I ask for? The only downside is the negative attitude towards recovery after an accident like mine. However, I think they gathered from day one that I wasn't having any of it.

The physios and consultants would use language like, "If this happens," or "If that happens," and I was having none of it. I'd put a stop to it instantly. I told them in my presence to say "when," not "if." I like a laugh and a joke, and I always did my best to be cheery and have a laugh. So when I initially came out with this phrase, they laughed and didn't take me seriously. When I repeated it a few times, they suddenly realised I was deadly serious. My future was in the hands of these people. I actually told them one day that if they said "if" whilst in my room, then they could leave. I wasn't surrounding myself in any negativity at all. I was going to win the hardest battle of my life.

My visualisation continued morning and night, and I would try my best at the physio sessions in hospital. They would say, "Do one more rep," and I would do two.

I would go in every day, ready for my session.

The physios would ask, "What would you like to do today, Keith?"

My reply would be, "To walk," said with a wry smile. I would sit at the end of the parallel bars and imagine myself walking along them. Bear in mind, at this time, I could only wiggle my big toe. Day in and day out, it was the same scenario. You have to see it to believe it. Yeah?

Four and a half months later, it was time for me to leave hospital. I had a little more movement in my legs and a little bit more strength in my arms. Things were improving. When I went to my final physio session, the physio got me up onto the parallel bars and essentially walked me along them. Although I managed the tiniest movement, I had just walked the length of the bars.

It was a momentous occasion. I went back to my room in tears of joy. I rang Christina and said to her, "I've just walked." I have it on film and often look back at it as the start. I knew I would get along those bars under my own steam one day.

Since I left hospital, I'm not going lie; it's been a struggle. In hospital, you're with a small community of people in a similar situation. When you come out into the real world and quickly realise that your old life has gone, it's hard to accept. I cannot do the simplest tasks like cook my own meals; my hands don't work properly, and I can't play football with my boys like I dreamed of.

However, I know I have a lot to be grateful for. I'm still here; I'm still me mentally, and I am very fortunate with the movement and recovery I've had so far. It's easy to focus on the negatives. Nevertheless, I work every day to make sure I'm focusing on the positives too and to live in the now.

I can't change the past, and I can't predict the future. I have to work on what I have right now, to enjoy my life to the fullest. I work as hard as I possibly can to make the future the best it possibly can be. There are days rehab goes well, and there are days it doesn't. There are days I'm absolutely shattered, and there are days I have lots of energy and feel great. I take the good with the bad.

I firmly believe those initial days in hospital, when I was mentally rebuilding pathways in my mind, had an impact on my healing.

So four and a half years later, here I am in my wheelchair dictating this, as it's hard to type. Every morning, I still visualise the signals from my brain going through the same pathways rerouting around the little side roads, down my fingers to help them work again. I've got to keep the focus. I've got to keep believing. And I've got to keep working hard to make me be the best version of myself I possibly can.

Can I walk the whole length of the bars yet? Not quite. I will though; watch me!

Keith is such an inspiration, and I believe he will walk unaided again because he is so determined and has enormous belief.

If you would like to follow Keith's journey, his Instagram profile is keith_dungait.

The next story is one my father has told us many times about when he was born.

My Father's Story

When my father, Chrysostomos, was born in July 1940 in the village of Yiallousa, Cyprus, he apparently had no heartbeat. The local priest told his mother and father that he was dead and they should bury him in a small grave in the garden. His Auntie Christina could not believe it, and as they were preparing to bury him, she picked him up and began to blow into his face whilst praying. Kyriakos, my father's father, started shouting at her to put him back. She wouldn't listen and kept blowing furiously into the baby's face.

How long it took is unclear, but it was most likely minutes before my father began to breathe again and, of course, lived. Everyone was elated.

A few weeks later, it became apparent that my father's arm was deformed, and Kyriakos began to pray to Saint Andrew on the day of the Virgin Mary's birth, 15 August. He promised that he would make a donation to the nearby church, Apostolos Andreas, if his son was cured. The next morning, his baby son stretched out his arm and was totally normal. Many years after, when my father had children, he named one of them after Saint Andrew, and that was me.

The following is the true account of a good friend of mine named Hayley, who used some of her natural healing abilities to overcome illness and heal herself.

Hayley's Story (Written in Her Own Words)

> I started having intermittent pains on my upper right torso. The sharp pains kept coming and going, and over the next few days, they got worse, bringing me to my knees. At first, I thought it might be trapped wind, but it lasted too long. It got so bad one evening, I felt like calling the doctor. However, I thought this would be an opportunity to put what I believe into practice. Over the last few years, I have learnt about the power of the mind and recently read a book about trapped emotions in the body which manifest as physical illness. I am a Quantum Holographic Echo Healing practitioner, so my first port of call was to establish if this pain was a trapped emotion. The children were in bed, so I went into the room next door, and using my pendulum to determine a yes or no answer, I asked if I had a trapped emotion in my body.

The answer was yes.

I then located where to in my body. The answer was my gall bladder. I cleared this stuck emotion with my intention and the pendulum by holding it close to the painful area. I then went back to bed and focused on my breathing. I could see in my mind's eye a mustard colour leaving my body as I breathed out.

The next day, I woke up, and the pain had gone. I decided to look more into the gall bladder and its location and was blown away when I realised it was in the same place as where my pain was. And the colour I saw must have been bile. I came to the conclusion I had gall stones, and when researching the symptoms, it was spot on with what I was experiencing. I'm now treating these naturally, and I haven't had any trouble since.

During the period of time documented in this book, I stumbled across the most amazing true stories, almost by accident. I hadn't seen any trailers or billboards advertising these movies or books. It was almost as if no one wanted us to see them. My problem with the world today is that only bad news gets through to us, as though they want us to see the most terrible things going on instead of the most amazing.

This true story is about a boy who became trapped under an icy lake for fifteen minutes but still lived.

The Impossible

On 19 January 2015, John Smith fell into an icy lake as he and his friends strolled along Lake St. Louis in Missouri, USA. The fourteen-year-old was submerged in the freezing water for more than fifteen minutes before paramedics managed to get him out. They attempted CPR for fifteen minutes at the scene before doctors continued for another twenty-seven minutes at SSM St. Joseph Hospital West. John showed no signs of life in the trauma room until his mother, Joyce Smith, began to pray loudly. Within minutes, his heart started beating again. Doctors then said he wouldn't survive for long and, if he did, he'd probably have brain damage.

John went on to make a full recovery and left the hospital less than a month later. Dr Jeremy Garrett, one of the doctors at the hospital, said, "It's a bona fide miracle," and was like nothing he had ever seen before.

Joyce Smith wrote a book about the event, which has gone on to become a movie called *Breakthrough*.

Death Is Not the End

I wanted to include this chapter because death is something many of us fear so much, it affects our living life. I was one of those people. However, it was during this time I came across true stories of people who'd had near-death experiences; this helped put my mind to rest. I also came across some great writings about death and what happens to us after we leave this earth. It was as if the universe was answering all my questions.

Just like the signs I already talked about, I believe the information I was led to regarding death was just another sign from God to help me to get through tough times. That's why I wanted to include it.

The sad thing about death is that we could spend every day worrying about it and never really live our life because of it. I've suffered panic attacks and anxiety for much of my life; I have come to realise that the predominant thought in my mind when I'm having a panic or anxiety attack is death-related. It's simple. I feel like I am about to die, and the attack gets worse.

This might come as a surprise to you, but my secret panic attack hack is to say the words, "So what if I die?" Saying these words has become like a switch that turns off the fear response, restores faith in my mind, and halts the attack in its tracks. Of course, this is because I fear death much less these days.

In the book *Conversations with God: An Uncommon Dialogue*, Neale Donald Walsch says, "The soul knows there is no great tragedy involved in leaving the body. Only in our earthy mind death is something to be feared.

"The soul is also clear that there is no great tragedy involved in leaving the body. In many ways, the tragedy is being in the body. So you have to understand, the soul sees this whole death thing differently. It, of course, sees the whole 'life thing' differently, too—and that is the source of much of the frustration and anxiety one feels in one's life. The frustration and anxiety comes from not listening to one's soul."

The one thing I began to do daily, which I believe has had a big impact on my life and helped me cope with anxiety issues, is to go within. I began to meditate and ask questions. By doing this, I believe I was able to speak to God, or to my higher self, and get answers.

Many of my questions were to do with illness and death, and what happens to us when we die. The following are some of the answers that came through:

When we die, we become spirit, and that's when life really begins. We are all knowing, and we are everywhere. Meaning, we hear everything, and we can go anywhere. Colours are brighter and more beautiful in heaven, with millions of hues and shades. Music and song are more amazing, with many more notes and sounds the human ear is unable to comprehend. The brightest light here on earth is a mere spark compared to the powerful, angelic and intense light in heaven our eyes have no problem looking directly at.

We can do anything we want to on the other side, from climbing Everest easily to flying high with the birds. We can go to any musical concert or show anywhere in the world. We can visit anyone in the living world and in the spirit world. We can go to any country faster than Superman and visit any other world or planet in the universe. Money is no issue; we can have anything we want, from a small cottage to the largest mansion.

Love is so much more powerful in heaven, and we have more than one soul mate. We can spend as much time with anyone in particular as we want, from five minutes to eternity.

Time in spirit world is not as we know it here. The past, present, and future can be experienced all at the same time. Our loved ones who pass before us here on earth don't have to wait years for us to arrive. For them, a hundred years is like one second. We can also visit the past, present, and future anytime we like. The human mind will never be able to understand this concept.

In heaven, we have the answers to everything we ever wanted to know, and there is no limit to what you can become in spirit world. There is no waiting, either. If you want to have anything in particular, you can have it or achieve it immediately because you are able to manifest anything instantly. The most amazing thing about the other side is that whatever it is you want, you can have it (as long as you or anyone else doesn't get hurt).

So start to imagine what you want and what you will do when you leave this earth, and know it will be the most amazing experience. Begin to associate death with all that is good instead of all that is bad. If you spend a moment to imagine being a grown human before you have to go through birth, wouldn't this scare the hell out of you? Did you spend time worrying about that? Of course not.

Most importantly, live this life on earth as though it is your one opportunity to achieve great things, to make a difference in your own life and to the lives of others. Go for that audition, even if you're not a trained actor; ask that girl out without regret, regardless of the outcome; take every opportunity that comes your way, without fear of failure; and be yourself, unapologetically.

I think the following quote from *Conversations with God* sums it all up quite nicely:

> To a doctor or a nurse, death is a failure. To a friend or relative, death is disaster. Only to the soul is death a relief—a release.

Daily Spiritual Actions

The following is a list of things I do each day to help keep me spiritually grounded. More importantly, in this fast-paced, nonstop world of technology, few people actually stop to appreciate life.

These daily actions can take less than fifteen minutes, but the benefits are incredible, mentally and physically.

My Daily Actions

1) I send love to everyone in the world.
2) I am grateful for each new day.
3) I aim to be present in every moment.
4) I meditate ten to twenty minutes.
5) I ask for guidance to help achieve my goals.
6) I visualise what I want to achieve.
7) I ask for spiritual signs and messages.
8) I ask for healing, mind and body.
9) I pray for peace on earth.
10) I say my affirmations.
11) I live a healthy, active lifestyle.

You don't need to start looking for messages or be obsessive about it. In fact, this has the opposite effect because you're not truly in harmony and trying too hard. Just believe, accept, and trust that you shall be taken care of and that the signs of reassurance will come to you when you're least expecting them.

Most of the things I practice in this book are from many other great spiritualists, and gradually, over the years, I have applied the things that work for me.

Be patient if your life is not currently going the way you would like it to. It will.

Trust the universe to deliver, open your mind, and believe in yourself.

Meditation

Some folks think meditation is a complicated act that only certain people can do. This isn't true. Anybody can do it, and I'll explain why in a moment.

It's often recommended that meditation is done twice a day, once in the morning and once in the evening, for twenty minutes each time. However, we all lead different lifestyles, and this is not always possible. So it's easier not to meditate at all.

My advice is, work out what times are best for you, and even if you manage five minutes once a day, it's better than nothing.

When I started meditating, it was mostly around five to ten minutes a day. Gradually, this increased because I felt the benefits and enjoyed it thoroughly. Now, I meditate for around fifteen to twenty minutes after breakfast. It's a time when I'm most alert.

A great book on meditation is Shakti Gawain's *Creative Visualisation*. It explains in depth what the benefits are, shows how we can change our lives for the better by thinking more positively, and has a number of meditations to suit everyone.

Meditation doesn't have to be a difficult act that we must be good at. This comes later. If you're new to it or not sure, just start by lying comfortably on your bed with your eyes closed. Perhaps just tune into the peace and quiet around you, or imagine a nice scene. Don't try too hard, and don't worry if you find it hard to imagine something. Just relax and accept everything. Below, I go through what I do when I meditate step-by-step, and then I've included five simple meditations you can try. Just go with the one you find easiest, or make up one of your own.

Meditating is good for the mind and body, as you probably already know, but it's also a good way to tune into the spirit world and help you notice the signs and support from the universe.

Here's the way I meditate every morning:

I relax by lying down on my bed facing the ceiling. I close my eyes and imagine all weight falling underside of my body. I take three deep breaths in through the nose and out from the mouth, whilst imagining breathing in healing, positive energy and breathing out doubt, fear, and negative energy. For instance, I breathe in love, healing energy, happiness, confidence, and courage. And I breathe out worry, stress, fear, and illness. This is totally up to you and takes around five minutes.

I will then send love and healing energy to myself (mind and body), to my family and friends, and often to the whole world and everyone in it. Sometimes, I may think of someone in particular at that moment. If so, I send special love to them because they may just need it, and that's the universe letting me know.

It's also important to mention that I send love to those I may not be getting on with. Especially if I think of them while meditating. Again, I believe this is God telling me to let go of any grudges because they simply do not serve me. And this helps me to be at peace. I also believe they receive the love, and I've found, over the years, it often mends relationships.

I thank the universe for the new day and the opportunity to make great things happen. I show gratitude for various things like my warm bed, my success, or whatever comes to mind at that moment.

I will then state my intentions, desires, and goals, and aim to visualise each of them. I imagine myself being the person I want to be: successful, positive, happy, healthy, and wealthy, for example.

Note, when doing this, be specific. Being successful is one thing, but how are you successful? Are you a dancer, a writer, an actor, or a top retailer? Make sure it's something you really want. Keep your mind on this for a few minutes.

If it's not easy to imagine because of where you are in life right now, make up some relevant affirmations that you can say to help create the images you want. For instance, if you want to be a great singer, say something like, "I am one of the greatest singers in the world." Don't say, "I will be" because that's what the universe will deliver. Use the words "I am" or "I have."

Once I've imagined my goals, I will then say some affirmations (like the ones in the next chapter) to help me combat negative thoughts and doubts, thus keeping away anxiety. Affirmations spoken time and time again have a hypnotic effect, thus allowing you to switch your mind to a positive state when you are thinking negative.

Finally, I will come back slowly to the room by counting down from five to one before I open my eyes and say, "Thank you," once again for the new day.

This won't be easy at first, but stick with it because it gets easier; trust me, it will make a big difference to your life.

Simple Meditations

Here are five of my favourite meditations relevant to this book.

There's one for healing, one to help with anxiety, one for attracting, one to meet your guardian angel, and one to speak to God or the universe.

Healing Meditation

Find a comfortable place to sit or lie down. Close your eyes and breathe in deeply through the nose and out from the mouth, slowly but naturally. Fill your lungs totally, holding the air in for a second or two, before exhaling. Focus on your belly rising as you breathe in before your chest expands, and aim to expel all air from your lungs when you breathe out. Repeat three to five times (or more if you want), and feel your whole body relax from top to bottom. Enjoy the feeling of total relaxation, and imagine all your weight falling underside of your body. Feel any tension in your body falling away.

Imagine that you have a tiny light shining in the centre of your body. Maybe it's a dot or seed-like light, and maybe it was planted there by your guardian angel. It could be a bright colour, like gold or yellow. Now, imagine it growing outwards and filling your whole body, and as it does, it heals you of any illness and also washes away any negative energy such as doubt, fear, worry, or stress. Imagine the beautiful, bright light filling your whole body and also radiating out of your body and healing others you love.

The powerful healing energy of the light could be touching certain parts of your body that need more healing, such as an achy back or bad belly. Visualise the light cleaning away aches and pains and any illness in your body. Enjoy the feeling of your body healing, and believe in the ability of your body to heal itself of absolutely anything.

Take time to visualise the healing light in your body for as long as you like, before counting back from 5 to 1 and opening your eyes. Give yourself a minute or two before getting up to allow your mind and body to fully return to the physical world.

Meditation to Help with Negative Thoughts and Fears

Find a comfortable place to sit or lie down. Close your eyes, and breathe in deeply through the nose and out from the mouth, slowly but naturally. Fill your lungs totally, holding the air in for a second or two, before exhaling. Focus on your belly rising as you breathe in before your chest expands, and aim to expel all air from your lungs when you breathe out. Repeat three to five times (or more if you want), and feel your whole body relax from top to bottom. Enjoy the feeling of total relaxation, and imagine all your weight falling underside of your body. Feel any tension in your body falling away.

Think of something that scares you or has you worried. If the scene comes easily into your mind, accept it without fighting against it. Let it come. Accept it, knowing you are strong enough to deal with it, and the universe or God is with you, protecting you with His powerful, enveloping energy. Imagine this scene or thing you fear as a black-and-white image, and imagine it moving away from you, getting smaller and smaller until it disappears.

Enjoy the feeling of any negative thoughts or fears disappearing from your life. Imagine some beautiful, positive scenes before counting back from 5-1, opening your eyes, and coming back to the room.

Meet Your Guardian Angel Meditation

Find a comfortable place to sit or lie down. Close your eyes and breathe in deeply through the nose and out from the mouth, slowly but naturally. Fill your lungs totally, holding the air in for a second or two, before exhaling. Focus on your belly rising as you breathe in before your chest expands, and aim to expel all air from your lungs when you breathe out. Repeat three to five times (or more if you want), and feel your whole body relax from top to bottom. Enjoy the feeling of total relaxation, and imagine all your weight falling underside of your body. Feel any tension in your body falling away.

Now I want you to imagine that your guardian angel is right there with you, as if it's a friend or family member keeping you company. She (or he) is there smiling at you and waiting for you to ask anything you wish. For instance, do you want to know what her name is? Or what he enjoys doing most? Have a conversation with your guardian angel, asking him anything you want. In the silence of the meditation, see if you can hear the answers or what your guardian is telling you. Trust that she is answering your question accurately, and feel comforted if it's anything to do with a worrying situation. Now, finish by asking your guardian angel for her help and support with something, anything. Know that your angel is always by your side, and speak to him as often as you like. Finish by sending love and gratitude to your guardian angel, and then count back 5-1, open your eyes, and come back to the room.

The Universe Speaks to You Meditation

Find a comfortable place to sit or lie down. Close your eyes, and breathe in deeply through the nose and out from the mouth, slowly but naturally. Fill your lungs totally, holding the air in for a second or two, before exhaling. Focus on your belly rising as you breathe in before your chest expands, and aim to expel all the air from your lungs when you breathe out. Repeat three to five times (or more if you want), and feel your whole body relax from top to bottom. Enjoy the feeling of total relaxation, and imagine all your weight falling underside of your body. Feel any tension in your body falling away.

Enjoy the total peace and quiet around you. Focus on the silence. Now become aware of the expansive space around you. Become aware of how much space there is all around you and high up into the universe. Space goes on forever. Become one with this space, and marvel in it. Imagine the infinite space brings a powerful energy with it and fills you up.

Now, in the total silence, mentally ask questions of the universe. And listen for answers. You won't hear a voice, but you may sense a response in the form of your intuition. For instance, "Universe, are you with me?" You may feel a response such as, "Yes, I am. I always am."

Be patient with this, as it may take many weeks to receive answers, but it eventually will happen. You will become more in tune with your intuition and the universe.

Enjoy this for as long as you like before counting back 5-1, opening your eyes, and coming back to the room.

I Am a Powerful Magnet Meditation

Find a comfortable place to sit or lie down. Start to breathe in as far into the belly and then into the chest as possible. Once you have breathed in fully, breathe out naturally and fully. Repeat three to five times, and feel your whole body relax from top to bottom. Enjoy the feeling of total relaxation, and imagine all your weight falling underside of your body.

Visualise becoming a magnet to all the things you greatly desire (or the one thing you greatly desire). Imagine that you attract everything you want because of your energy, similar to a magnet. So take time to imagine this and feel that you are attracting only the things you want. Enjoy this for a while.

Now, similarly to attracting, a magnet also repels like poles. Visualise repelling anything you don't need in your life. Imagine that certain negativity does not touch you or even get close to you because you repel it with your only-positive energy.

Enjoy attracting only what you want in your life for a few moments before saying the following affirmation three or more times:

"I am a _____ magnet." Fill in the blank word with whatever you want, such as good health or money. Count back 5-1, open your eyes, and come back to the room.

Affirmations

I have included affirmations in the book because they have helped me to overcome anxiety and depression. When you find yourself thinking negatively, replace those thoughts with positive affirmations like the ones below. Or choose your own.

I recommend you choose those that feel right for you and say them daily.

> My mind is calm, and I think positive thoughts at all times and in all situations.
>
> I am full of radiant good health, healing energy, vitality, and a strong immune system.
>
> I accept everything that happens to me. I trust my mind, body, and soul to deal with it naturally, and I am at total peace with myself.
>
> I surrender to God and know that whatever happens, it is all for the best.
>
> God, His saints, my guardian angels, and my spirit guides protect me, heal me, guide me in the right direction, and help to create miracles and other great things in and around my life now.
>
> Love comes easily and frequently, and I am so happy and grateful.
>
> Perfect health comes easily, and I am so happy and grateful.
>
> Success comes easily and frequently, and I am so happy and grateful.
>
> Money comes easily and frequently, and I am so happy and grateful.

A brilliant book that helps deal with negative self-talk is *What to Say When You Talk to Yourself* by Shad Helmstetter.

The best time to say affirmations is after a relaxation or meditation session.

Prayer

I believe one of the biggest challenges of our modern world is getting humankind to agree. It's in our nature to disagree, argue, judge, criticise, blame, hate, and fight. The one thing we could do, however, is try to understand each other and make peace.

I was brought up as a Greek Orthodox and still follow this religion (although not strictly). And as with all religions, we are taught to pray. But I have to be totally honest, before, I wasn't a big believer of praying, even though I did it a lot. I never really believed it worked. Or if anyone was actually listening.

However, along with everything that has happened, things that have led me to write this book, my belief has totally changed. Apart from my personal experiences, I have read a number of books, watched films, and heard stories of miracles that have happened. The one common factor every time is prayer; there was a strong network of people praying in the background.

This is certainly evident in true stories such as "Miracles from Heaven," "Dying to Be Me," "Heaven Is for Real," "The Impossible," and "Thai Cave Rescue."

You don't have to be religious to pray. I believe the universe is always listening; if you don't like the word *pray*, just use the word "ask." "I ask for peace," for instance. But say it with real intent and desire.

Spiritual References and Resources

The Myrrh-Leaking Icon from Hawaii, https://www.youtube.com/watch?v=E1shRL859eY (YouTube Video)

Miracles from Heaven (book and film)

Dying to Be Me, by Anita Moorjani (book)

The Ten Secrets of Heaven, by Theresa Cheung (book)

Angel Numbers 101, by Doreen Virtue (book)

Conversations with God, by Neale Donald Walsch (book series)

Rhian the Psychic Reader, Psychicmaiden (Facebook page)

The Power, by Rhonda Byrne (book)

The Secret, by Rhonda Byrne (book)

Angels in My Hair, by Lorna Byrne (book)

Prayers from the Heart, by Lorna Byrne (book)

The Seven Spiritual Laws of Success, by Deepak Chopra (book)

Creative Visualisation, by Shakti Gawain (book)

Heaven Is for Real, by Todd Burpo (book and film)

"The Girl Who Paints Heaven," Akaine Kramerik (www.YouTube.com)

What To Say When You Talk to Yourself, by Shad Helmstetter (book)

Heal, by Kelly Noonan Gores (book and documentary)

Joe Dispenza (YouTube)

Breakthrough (film based on the book *The Impossible,* by Joyce Smith)

Thai Boys Rescue (film)

Jo Cantle, transformational coach (Facebook.com/JoCantle)

Dare: The New Way to End Anxiety and Stop Panic Attacks Fast, by Barry McDonagh (Audible book)

Acknowledgements

I am truly grateful to my family and friends for their help and support of this book, and for their honest feedback.

Thank you also to those who allowed me to include their stories in the book.

I would like to thank the following people for their input, help, support, and inspiration during the writing of the book. And for giving me the belief that this book could actually be something of a reality.

In no particular order:

Jodie Hopkin, Hayley Ryan, Jo Cantle, Culide Dirk, Rhian Godwin, Jonathan Edwards, Taylor Harding, Jaye Swift, Wayne Spear, Beverly Dillon, Jo Tsenti, Barry Hajilambi, Yianoulla Dixon, Darren Tyson, Angela Peart, Andria Andreou, Angelo Aviles, Charlotte Goodby, Holly Mcgillivray.

I'm pretty sure I've missed someone, but please know, I am truly grateful to each and every one who believed in this project.

I would especially also like to thank my immediate family for their continuous belief and support: Mum, Dad, Joanna, Giggs, Karin, Chris, Demetri, and Lucy.

Thank you, everyone. xxx

Thank You

Thank you for purchasing this book. I do hope you have found it of value. Please go to the book on Amazon and add a small review. This will only take a moment and helps others when they are looking at the book. And also, the feedback helps me to improve further editions.

Many Best Wishes!

Andrew Kanias has written several feature-length screenplays and earned himself a trial-write for a top TV soap. He has always been passionate about health and wellness and is a big believer in self-help and taking charge of your own life. He suffered a nervous breakdown in 1993 and has battled anxiety. He wrote this book to help others who are struggling and to encourage them to consider that the universe (or God) is always there with us.

What Have You Seen?

Do You Have a Story?

I believe there are so many stories of inspiration out there that the world needs to hear. The universe wants to communicate.

Do you have a story which is obvious guidance from God and the universe?

Have you experienced what can only be explained as a miracle?

Please email your story to TheSecretSigns@hotmail.com, and it will be published on our social media pages.

I look forward to hearing from you soon.

What Have You Seen?

_____

_____

_____

_____

_____

_____

_____

_____

_____

_____

_____

_____

_____

What Have You Seen?

9781982285999